Julia Goodfellow-

111 Places
in Swansea
That You
Shouldn't Miss

111

emons:

To David Taylor, for introducing me to the '111 Places' books

Bibliographical information of the Deutsche Nationalbibliothek
The Deutsche Nationalbibliothek lists this publication in
the Deutsche Nationalbibliografie; detailed bibliographical data
are available on the internet at http://dnb.d-nb.de.

© Emons Verlag GmbH
All rights reserved
© Photographs by Julia Goodfellow-Smith, except:
Cu Mumbles (ch. 28): Mike Goodfellow-Smith
© Cover icon: shutterstock.com/Malikov Aleksandr
Layout: Eva Kraskes, based on a design
by Lübbeke | Naumann | Thoben
Maps: altancicek.design, www.altancicek.de
Basic cartographical information from Openstreetmap,
© OpenStreetMap-Mitwirkende, OdbL
Edited by: Tania Taylor
Printing and binding: Grafisches Centrum Cuno, Calbe
Printed in Germany 2024
ISBN 978-3-7408-2065-7
First edition

Guidebooks for Locals & Experienced Travellers
Join us in uncovering new places around the world at
www.111places.com

Foreword

Swansea is sometimes overlooked and underestimated. In this book, I hope to remove its cloak of modesty and reveal its true spirit.

Nestled between green hills and the shimmering sea, Swansea offers breathtaking vistas at every turn. The landscape inland offers a beautiful tapestry of forests, rivers and moors. The coastline mirrors this variety. It has limestone cliffs with caves on the south side of the Gower, mudflats on the north, sheltered swimming beaches, wild surfing beaches and many acres of dunes. The Gower Peninsula was deservedly the first place in the UK to become designated as an 'Area of Outstanding Natural Beauty'.

Humans have lived in this area for several millennia. Our Bronze and Iron Age ancestors built tombs and hill forts here, the Romans built villas and forts, and the Normans built castles, manor houses and abbeys. The area's rich natural resources, particularly coal, meant that Swansea was the birthplace of the Industrial Revolution. The city's industrial heyday is over, and many of the city's historic buildings were destroyed in a three-day blitz in February 1941, but the city's spirit lives on.

As you embark on this journey through Swansea's 111 most fascinating places, prepare to be surprised, delighted and inspired. From ancient ruins to cutting-edge cultural venues, from sporting triumphs to literary landmarks, each entry unveils a new facet of the city's character. Whether you're a lifelong resident or curious visitor, this book promises to reshape your understanding of the Swansea area and ignite your appreciation for its fascinating life.

This book explores the area's rich cultural and natural heritage. As I have explored its streets and talked to its people, my connection to my newly adopted home has deepened. Now, it is my great pleasure to share this love with you. I hope you enjoy the result as much as I enjoyed writing it.

111 Places

1　Aberavon Whale

Having a whale of a time

Aberavon Sands is not where you would expect to see a blue whale, with penguins standing guard on icebergs nearby. While real whales and penguins are threatened by environmental pollution, noisy seas and global heating, these sculptures were once threatened by the 'need' for car parking. Local children were up in arms about the possibility of losing their park, so they started a petition and met with the council leader to protest. They succeeded in their quest to save the sculptures, which means that their children can now play on and around these models, as they once did. The children's action demonstrated how effective grassroots activism can be, as well as the importance of standing up for what you believe in, whatever your age.

Real whales do occasionally stray into Swansea Bay, although sadly, most don't seem to have survived, thanks to the usefulness of whale oil. In 1864, two whales were seen near Mumbles Head. One was killed and pulled ashore in Oystermouth, and the other made it round to the mouth of the River Tawe before being shot and attached to the shore. Once the tide retreated, the whale was stranded, providing a spectacle for local people, who paid a penny apiece to see it. Before long, it was controversially claimed by the Duke of Beaufort, cut up and rendered for oil. For all of the issues associated with the use of fossil fuels now, their discovery did at least stop us from slaughtering millions of whales for their oil.

In 1986, the International Whaling Commission banned commercial whaling. Although some countries have chosen to step away from that agreement, it has resulted in several species starting to recover from the brink of extinction. Now, the commission can focus on how to make whale-watching sustainable and reducing accidental harm such as ship strikes, entanglement in nets and ocean noise, thus ensuring the future of these magnificent beasts.

Address The Princess Margaret Way, Port Talbot, SA12 6QN | Getting there Train to Port Talbot Parkway, then a 40-minute walk; bus to Port Talbot Bus Station, then a 30-minute walk; on-street parking nearby | Hours Accessible 24 hours | Tip If you would like to see wild cetaceans, the Gower Peninsula is a good place to go. Boat trips are available from Oxwich Bay.

2 Aberdarcy Public Library
Only Two Can Play

Imagine Swansea a few years after World War II, a provincial town that had suffered from severe bombing and whose industry was in major decline. It did not become a city until 1969 and was nothing like the vibrant place it is today. Then imagine what a stir must have been created when Kingsley Amis arrived in 1949, fresh from gaining a first-class honours degree at Oxford, to take up a junior lecturing position at Swansea University. By all accounts, he was a colourful character at work and home, and his parties were legendary, providing a welcome distraction from the challenges of post-war reconstruction.

His first novel *Lucky Jim* was published five years after arriving, followed the next year by *That Uncertain Feeling*. Both were comedies, the first set in a provincial university, the second in a Welsh seaside town. It can only be assumed that both were inspired by his life in Swansea. *That Uncertain Feeling* was made into a film in 1962, with a title change to *Only Two Can Play*. Peter Sellers was cast into the leading role of the librarian who finds himself the subject of the attentions of a powerful predatory woman who can influence his chances of promotion. The film was nominated for a BAFTA, and Kingsley Amis became a celebrity author. Much of *Only Two Can Play* was filmed in Swansea, and the Glynn Vivian Art Gallery was transformed into Aberdarcy Public Library.

Kingsley Amis lived in Swansea for 12 years and claimed that his best work was written while here. Overall, he wrote over 20 novels, poetry, non-fiction, memoir and television and radio scripts. In 1985, he was awarded an Honorary Fellowship of Swansea University. In 1986, he won the Booker Prize for *The Old Devils*, which was also set in Swansea, although by the time he wrote it, he had been gone for a while. In 1990, he was knighted and became Sir Kingsley Amis.

Address Glynn Vivian Art Gallery, Alexandra Road, Swansea, SA1 5DZ, www.glynnvivian.co.uk | **Getting there** Bus 16 to Orchard Street; a short walk from Swansea railway station | **Hours** Viewable from the outside 24 hours; gallery Tue – Sun 10am – 4.30pm | **Tip** The actual library in Swansea is in a somewhat less attractive, modern building down by the seafront.

3   Abertawe Barrage
Rising to the challenge

This barrier across the River Tawe is a late 20th-century addition, built to create a larger marina. Blocking a river can be devastating to local wildlife, as muddy banks full of inter-tidal organisms become permanently submerged and migrating fish find an insurmountable barrier between them and their spawning grounds. Since the 18th century, engineers have been working on a solution to the fish migration issue. The Abertawe Barrage uses the most popular version of a fish pass – a 'ladder' – between the lock and the barrage itself. A series of stepped pools allows fish to jump up from the bay to the river, one step at a time, without exhausting themselves. The trick is to make the steps just the right size, with enough water flow to attract the fish but not so much that they are exhausted before they have reached the top. The next challenge is to keep them alive in the marina.

Seawater flows over the top of the barrage at high tide. It holds less oxygen than fresh water, and because it's also heavier, it gets trapped behind the barrier. For a while, the lack of oxygen made the river inhospitable for fish, so the marina is now aerated. This stirs up the water and raises oxygen levels. The method was so successful that the same technology was deployed for the far larger barrage across Cardiff Bay. Look out for the rings of bubbles rising to the surface.

No real solution has yet been found to the damage caused by permanently submerging mudflats.

There are, of course, also opportunities with any scheme like this. The steady flow of water from the river is used to generate hydropower. This power is used to pump water back into the basin when required and to work the lock, which is large enough for small fishing vessels to pass through. The marina was also expanded, creating an area that is popular for waterside dining and strolling.

Address Swansea, SA1 1FZ | Getting there A 20-minute walk from Swansea railway station; bus 7 to Swansea Marina; nearest parking next to Marina Park at the end of Trawler Road | Hours Accessible 24 hours | Tip There is a café right next to the lock, which is next to the barrage. If you wait for a while, you might see one of the fishing fleet pass through the lock.

4 The Admiral's Tower
A bird's-eye view

When retired Admiral Algernon Walker Heneage inherited Clyne Castle from his mother's family in 1921, he added her surname to his. This resulted in a triple-barrelled surname; he became Admiral Algernon Walker-Heneage-Vivian. He was clearly a man who did not do things by halves, as evidenced by his garden as well as his name. The pleasure grounds he developed are now known as Clyne Gardens, owned by Swansea City Council, and open to the public.

The admiral planted a profusion of rhododendrons and azaleas. The gardens now house national collections of these, enkianthus and pieris. In spring, there is a riot of shape and colour as the garden bursts into flower, especially in the area nearest to the Woodman pub. The Admiral's tower is most easily found by entering the park near the pub, following a path down to the stream on the left, and then following the stream uphill.

Not content with admiring his rhododendrons from eye height, he built this five-metre-tall construction to get a close-up view of the flowers. A spiral staircase runs up the outside of the tower, and a small platform at the top snugly fits two people.

Further up the wooded valley is a garden with a pool and cascade. The Japanese bridge across the stream is a striking scarlet and white – a replica of the original the admiral installed. A superb handkerchief tree stands on the downhill side of the bridge. When in bloom, the creamy flower bracts make it look like it has hundreds of handkerchiefs draped from it. Steps rise from the far side of the bridge, and further uphill in that direction, the view opens out east across the city and Swansea Bay.

Clyne Castle is the far side of the grassy sward, flanked by some enormous Monterey Pines with branches that reach down to the ground. With the castle to the left, the entrance to the park is downhill and round to the right.

Address Mayals, Swansea, SA3 5BA, www.swansea.gov.uk/clyne | Getting there Buses 2, 2A, 2B, 3, 3A, 14, 14A, 37 to Woodman pub; parking next to Woodman pub | Hours Accessible 24 hours | Tip Clyne Valley Country Park adjoins Clyne Gardens and has extensive footpaths and cycleways through native woodland that has been reclaimed from an old industrial site.

5 Amy Dillwyn's Grave
'A man of business'

(Elizabeth) Amy Dillwyn defied Victorian convention. She dressed and behaved in what was considered a masculine way, rather than conforming to the notion that women should be pretty and quiet. She wrote novels with 'tomboy' protagonists and women with fluid sexuality, which seem to have drawn on her own experience of life. She wrote about issues of social justice from the perspective of the working class and railed against the upper class to which she belonged.

This was already pretty revolutionary in Victorian Britain, but when her father died in 1892, Amy, by then in her late 40s, really came into her own. Born into a wealthy industrial and political family, she grew up and lived in her family mansion and ran the house and estate. Inheritance laws at the time were skewed in favour of men, so she did not inherit her home when her father died. What she did inherit, though, were her father's loss-making spelter works (a type of cheap alloy) and £100,000 of debt, the equivalent of around £8 million today. She could have declared bankruptcy. Instead, she rented cheap lodgings and ran the business herself. Within 10 years, she managed to make a profit, pay off the creditors and buy herself a house in Mumbles, where she lived until she died. During this period, she called herself 'a man of business', highlighting that she was the equal of men despite being desperately discriminated against for being a woman.

In the early 20th century, Amy Dillwyn was also an early and ardent member of the women's suffrage movement, supporting the National Union of Women's Suffrage Societies and helping striking women to gain improved working conditions. She was not to be trifled with and blazed a path for women's emancipation.

E. Amy Dillwyn lived until she was 90. Her ashes are buried under this gravestone in St Paul's and Holy Trinity Church, Sketty.

Address De-la-Beche Road, Sketty, Swansea, SA2 9AR | Getting there Various buses to Sketty Cross; on-street parking nearby | Hours Accessible 24 hours | Tip There are two blue plaques dedicated to Amy Dillwyn in Swansea – one on her former home in Mumbles and one on the waterfront at Blackpill.

6 Arthur's Stone
David vs. Goliath?

Although the King Arthur Hotel in nearby Reynoldston displays a sword in its reception, Arthur's Stone (known as 'Maen Ceti' in Welsh – 'Ceti's stone') has no known association with the mythological king. The name, thought to have been in everyday use for over 300 years, refers instead to Arthur from Llanelli, a giant who threw a pebble from his shoe in irritation. It landed on Cefn Bryn, the ridge that runs along the Gower Peninsula. That pebble is, in fact, a conglomerate boulder of some size, composed of smaller rocks and pebbles that have been cemented together over millions of years. It is thought to weigh over 30 tonnes and was most likely dropped by a retreating glacier.

It now balances rather precariously above ground, with a double chamber beneath. In the distant past, our ancestors dug under the boulder and propped it up with other rocks. It is likely to have been a tomb. In such a position, with views across the Loughor estuary and north across Wales, and with such effort having gone into creating it, it must have provided a final resting place for someone of high status. The sides of the tomb are now open but were probably filled in with stones and possibly turf when it was created. The entire structure forms a circle that is 23 metres across.

Arthur's Stone was once much larger than it is now, as some of it has split off and sits on the ground. In around 1800, the historian and promoter of the Eisteddfod, Iolo Morganwg, wrote that this was the work of St David. He claims that the saint struck the stone with his sword to crack it and thus prove that the site was not sacred, then commanded water to spring from under the tomb. Although the ground often does hold water, Iolo is believed to have embellished the story to promote Welsh culture, as he was known to mix historical facts with romantic stories for the greater good.

Address North of the road between Reynoldston and Cillibion | Getting there Parking available 700 metres east of Reynoldston | Hours Accessible 24 hours | Tip There are also two significant burial chambers on the east side of Rhossili Down (Sweyne's Howes), although neither is as large as Arthur's Stone.

7 _ Battle of Gower
When the land ran red

The history of the Battle of Gower can be traced back to the Norman Invasion in 1066. After winning the Battle of Hastings, it only took a few years for the Normans to seize control of the whole of England, but their expansion into Wales proved to be much more challenging. Although they quickly took the south coast of Wales, the local Welsh rulers were not too happy about this and kept an eye out for opportunities to regain control over their country.

Back in England, things became rather hairy after the death of King Henry I. His only legitimate son pre-deceased him, and he was keen for his daughter, Empress Matilda, to succeed to the throne. When Henry I died on 2 December, 1135, a power struggle ensued between Matilda and her cousin Stephen. This proved to be a big distraction for the Norman invaders and provided just the opportunity that the ousted local rulers had sought. Only one month after the king's death, Welsh rebels attacked the Anglo-Norman army at the Battle of Gower, also known as the Battle of Llwchwr.

Much to the Anglo-Normans' surprise, they suffered heavy losses and were defeated. The battlefield was on Carn Goch Common, *goch* meaning 'red' in Welsh; this is where the land turned red with the blood of the vanquished. According to a contemporary account, 516 men lost their lives. Their bodies were 'horribly scattered among the fields and eaten up by wolves'.

This victory boosted the Welsh rebels' confidence and inspired a series of challenges to Norman rule. Ultimately, it was another 150 years before the whole of Wales was conquered. Luckily, there are no marauding wolves or soldiers left on the battlefield site. Instead, a stone memorial stands in honour of the fallen and the important place this battle holds in the history of Wales. A signpost from the road indicates the sometimes-boggy route across the common to the memorial stone.

Address Hospital Road, Loughor | Getting there Bus 111 to Hospital Road; the field entrance is on Hospital Road between the B 4560 and the A 484 | Hours Unrestricted | Tip If you are interested in the history of the Swansea area, the staff at Swansea Central Library have a wealth of information at their fingertips (Oystermouth Road, SA1 3SN).

8 Beach House Restaurant
From coal to cuisine

Despite its name, Beach House has never been a beach house. Built around 1800, it was the coal house for the Penrice Estate, used to store fuel for heating. After World War II ended, tourism started to grow on Gower, and the estate saw the potential for an alternative use. The coal was removed, and the building was converted into a café and then a watersports centre. The watersports centre closed, and the structure sat unused and slowly decaying, creating an eyesore at one end of Oxwich Bay.

In 2016, this somewhat sad-looking building was reimagined into the high-end restaurant it is today. It retains its industrial vibe, but the use could not be any further removed from that it was built for. Now, it is light and airy, with windows that look out over the bay. Diners on the terrace are treated to stunning views. To the east, the sandy beach stretches over two miles to the dramatic limestone peaks of Three Cliffs Bay and beyond. To the west, trees cling to the cliffs that are occasionally subject to rock falls, and the ancient sanctuary of St Illtyd's Church looks benevolently across the sands. Beach House is the only Michelin-starred restaurant in the area and specialises in using locally sourced, seasonal ingredients. Locals fish for lobster and seabass, and walk straight up the beach into the kitchen with their catch – the carbon footprint can be measured in food steps rather than food miles. The restaurant even tells you which boat to look out for, bringing the catch in. Other notable ingredients include Gower Salt Marsh Lamb, laverbread (a dish made from seaweed) and Brefu Bach cheese.

Although not lifeguarded, the bay is also a popular place for swimming and watersports, with a soft sandy beach backed by rolling dunes and hills. It is also popular with dog walkers, as dogs are allowed on the beach year-round and the Wales Coast Path wends through the dunes.

Address Oxwich Beach, Gower, Swansea, SA3 1LS, www.beachhouseoxwich.co.uk, reservations@beachhouseoxwich.co.uk | Getting there Bus 117 to Oxwich Cross; parking adjacent to beach | Hours See website for details | Tip The café with tables on the sand a little further along the beach offers a dining experience that is more financially accessible for many.

9 _ The Big Apple
A cider a day keeps the doctor away

These days, people joke about a glass of wine being one of their 'five a day' fruit and vegetable portions because it is made from grapes. It seems this joke has been around for the best part of a century. Back in the 1930s, Cidatone had 'Drink your apple a day' painted on the side of their distinctive apple-shaped kiosk between Bracelet Bay and Mumbles Pier. Although little is known about the company, there is an assumption that they sold cider rather than apple juice and that this was their inducement to customers to drink themselves healthy. Funnily enough, there is no mention of any possible adverse effects of drinking cider on a hot summer's day.

The structure, made from a single sphere of pre-stressed concrete, has been a feature of Mumbles and Bracelet Bay since the early 1930s and, as the last of its kind, is now a listed building. Over the years, it has seen some changes, although the iconic shape has remained the same. In 2009, a car drove into it, creating a lot of damage. Luckily, after some head-scratching, the owner worked out how to repair it and return it to use. As you see in this photo, it is usually painted red and green, but it was once vandalised and re-painted orange. 'The Big Pumpkin' doesn't have such a great ring to it, though, so it was soon returned to its usual colours.

The slogan is no longer on the side; instead, it sports a picture of an ice cream, reflecting its most recent use. The Big Apple is placed prominently in view for anyone arriving at Bracelet Bay through the cutting from Swansea. It is much loved by the people of the city who have visited the bay since childhood and bought ice cream, buckets and spades from the kiosk. It is also clearly visible from the restaurant on the far side of the bay, perhaps tempting diners to take a post-prandial walk around the cliffs. With ice cream in hand, they can then head up onto Mumbles Point to enjoy the view over the lighthouse, pier, Swansea Bay and the Bristol Channel.

Address Bracelet Bay Car Park, Mumbles Road, Mumbles, SA3 4JT | Getting there Bus 2A, 2B, 3A to Mumbles Pier Head Hotel; paid parking in car park | Hours Viewable from the outside only | Tip Mumbles Fine Wines (524 Mumbles Road) sells a good selection of Welsh ciders.

10 Bluepool Corner

A rock-solid day out

Bluepool Corner is best known for the deep rock pool on the beach. With its vertical sides and sandy bottom way below the level of the beach, this deep pool, surrounded by rugged, weathered rocks, is a perfect place to cool off on a hot summer day and is loved by children who throw themselves in from on high. There are several caves along the bay, and at the far end, you will see Three Chimneys Arch, an unusual triangular-shaped rock formation you can scramble through at low tide.

Just beyond the arch, human remains were found in Three Chimneys Cave (also known as Culver Hole) when it was excavated in the early 20th century. During the Beaker period of the early Bronze Age, named for the distinctive clay drinking vessels found at many burial sites, bodies were left in open graves, and the bones were either rearranged or moved later. It is thought that Three Chimneys Cave was used as an ossuary during and after this period, possibly for the community that lived on Burry Holms, the island a short distance to the south west of this point. Local people continued to use the cave for rituals up to a century ago, perhaps drawn by a sense of wonder at the power of nature and the insignificance of people in comparison.

On a lighter note, the bay in front of the beach is part of a Special Protection Area, as it is one of the most important sites in the British Isles for overwintering common scoters. Keep an eye out for flocks of a black (male) or dark brown (female) duck smaller than a mallard, with a pointed tail. They dive with a small forward jump and often rise up on their tails to exercise their wings. The shallow waters of the bay also attract flocks of black and white oystercatchers parading along the edge of the shore and teal, and if you're lucky in winter, you might see the ghostly swaying of a murmuration of starlings.

Address On the coast near Llangennith | **Getting there** Park at Broughton Farm Caravan Park, SA3 1JL, and walk left along the cliffs | **Hours** Accessible 24 hours, although there's no beach at high tide | **Tip** There is another natural arch on Worm's Head. Travel to Rhossili and it's an adventurous walk across to the island at low tide.

11 Brangwyn Hall
Raising the roof

Everyone in Swansea knows the Brangwyn Hall – by sight, at least. Its iconic 1930s art deco clocktower dominates the skyline. The tower is decorated with galley prows, celebrating the legend of Swansea's Viking past. The hall is a renowned concert venue and the city's guildhall. It was built at a time of economic depression, and its construction provided valuable jobs during this period.

The Hall is decorated with a series of panels painted by Sir Frank Brangwyn. The 'British Empire Panels' were commissioned for the Royal Gallery in the House of Lords to commemorate World War I. The paintings depict people, habitats and animals from across the British Empire, often in a fantastical form. Before the panels were completed, two of the project's prominent supporters died, and Brangwyn had to show the five panels that were finished in the Royal Gallery. Some influential people were horrified; the panels were considered too vulgar for such an august place. The commission was declined, although one of the supporting peers' heirs paid for the panels to be finished.

With their future uncertain, the panels were shown at the Ideal Home Exhibition in 1933, and both Cardiff and Swansea councils took a shine to them. Swansea secured the deal, based on the promise to show them in the new guildhall. The building was not yet finished, so the roof height was increased to fit the panels in.

A few months before the hall was ready to open, the executors of Sir Griffith Thomas offered the council £3000 towards the cost of an organ. At the time, renowned organ builders Willis were installing organs for cathedrals, such as Westminster. A second-hand Willis organ was procured – an instrument of far better quality than could have been hoped for, for what was then still a provincial town. Between the architecture, the panels and the organ, the Brangwyn Hall offers a unique venue, whatever the occasion.

Address Guildhall, Swansea, SA1 4PE, +44 (0)1792 635432, www.brangwyn.co.uk |
Getting there Bus to Swansea Crown Court or The Slip; parking at The Baths car park |
Hours See website for performance schedule; otherwise, open by appointment only |
Tip Swansea now has another major concert and entertainment space: Swansea Arena
(www.swansea-arena.co.uk).

12 Broad Pool Nature Reserve

Scorpions and stick insects

Many people will have driven past Broad Pool on their way to Arthur's Stone or the King Arthur Hotel at Reynoldston and admired the reflections from its dark surface.

Stop awhile, and more will come to light. The first thing you might notice in summer is the horseflies – beware of their vicious bites! It is worth persisting, though. Fourteen different dragonfly species come to the pool to drink. Often, all you will see is a colourful body darting around, hunting. Unusually, dragonflies can fly backwards as well as forwards, and their top speed is 54 kilometres an hour. No wonder they are so difficult to keep track of! Slower-moving grazing animals can also often be spotted congregating around the pool. Please be aware that the ponies are semi-feral and sometimes kick.

Although shallow, the pool rarely dries up and is an important breeding site for amphibians. It is also home to both water stick insects and water scorpions. The water scorpion looks like its poisonous namesake, but the tail is not used to sting – it is a snorkel used for breathing underwater. The water scorpion does not like to swim, so it lurks underneath leaves at the water's edge, waiting to pounce on unsuspecting prey. A water scorpion bite may not be very painful to humans but is likely to prove deadly for a tadpole or small fish. The water stick insect is related to the water scorpion and hunts in a similar way. Look out for something that resembles a mantis, lying in wait in the shallows.

Uncommon in South Wales, lesser marshwort and alternate flowered milfoil both grow in the pool. The other plant you will notice in summer is the fringed water lily, which was introduced in the 1960s and can be very invasive.

In winter, the pool is an excellent place to see herons patiently waiting for prey, or little grebes as they bob up from a dive.

Address West side of the road between Reynoldston and Cillibion | **Getting there** There is a small space to park at the side of the road adjacent to the pool | **Hours** Accessible 24 hours | **Tip** If you fancy a picnic nearby, continue to the car park about 2.25 kilometres closer to Reynoldston. Head uphill to the ridge of Cefn Bryn for great views over the Bristol Channel to the south and Loughor Estuary to the north.

13 Brynteg Petting Farm
A calming cwtch

Spending time in nature and with animals has a myriad of health benefits. Interacting with friendly animals increases the brain chemicals serotonin and dopamine, which improve mood and generate a feeling of calm. For people with mental health challenges, petting, feeding and cwtching animals can boost self-confidence and self-esteem while also reducing depression and loneliness. (*Cwtch* is a Welsh word that rhymes with 'butch' and is often used by Welsh people when they are speaking English because there is no direct translation. In this context, it is a special sort of hug – one that is homely and safe.) Heart health can also be impacted as blood pressure drops and the heart slows. In addition, this sort of activity has been shown to generate an improvement in dementia-related symptoms. Here, too, studies show that pet therapy improves mood, provides a calming effect and reduces challenging behaviour such as agitation and aggression.

Brynteg Farm welcomes groups who simply want to enjoy spending time with the animals or who want to generate some therapeutic benefit for their members. Everyone who visits has the opportunity to pet and feed the animals, and in the right weather conditions, it may be possible to ride one of the ponies. Even people scared to touch smaller animals generally love spending time with the horses. Although these animals are large, they exude a sense of calm that is catching. All the animals on the farm have been rescued from places where they have not been given the living conditions and love they deserve. Once they arrive at Brynteg Farm, they are given plenty of loving attention, so they are all happy to be petted. That is their job, after all!

The time we spend with animals can improve their quality of life as well as our own. Brynteg Farm provides a fantastic opportunity to do just that, with animals that are both loved and loving.

Address Pen Coed Isaf Road, Bynea, SA14 9TW, +44 (0)7967 105899, www.bryntegfarm.co.uk | Getting there Bus 111 to Brynhelyg Nursing Home; train to Bynea; both followed by a 10-minute walk uphill; limited parking on street and site | Hours By appointment only | Tip Cross the bridge at Loughor, turn left and left again for an easy walk along the river with beautiful views across the water.

14 Cadle Heath

A marvellous mosaic

If you only visit Fforestfach to dash into one of the superstores, you might be surprised at what you find on the hills behind the shops. Cadle Heath is a fantastic example of urban heathland, just metres from this busy retail area. It is a mix of wet heathland, grassland, ponds, scrub and wetland, providing a variety of habitats for wildlife, including dragonflies, damselflies, frogs and birds.

In summer, look out for the pink or purple spires of southern marsh orchids or the delicate pink flowers of heather on their somewhat less delicate, scratchy stems. Whorled caraway reaches to thigh height, where its white and purple flowers seem to explode from the tip of the stem. This plant is relatively common on old meadows in south-west Wales but rare across the UK as a whole. Wood bitter vetch grows here, too, one of only two sites in West Glamorgan where it does. It is also known as 'upright vetch' because it can grow to 60cm tall. It is a member of the pea family, with stems of up to 20 drooping pink flowers over the summer months.

All of these plants attract birds and insects. Wood bitter vetch is thought to be pollinated by specialist bumble bees with particularly long tongues. Can you see any buzzing around? Keep an eye open, too, for the marsh fritillary butterflies, with the distinctive bright orange, brown and yellow chequerboard pattern on their wings. Looking closely, you might notice that they have hairy bodies and stripey antennae with orange tips. This is one of our most threatened butterfly species, so it is worth protecting! In turn, insects attract birds, and 31 species have been spotted here.

The nature reserve is managed by the council, with help from volunteers from Swansea Community Farm, and has been granted a Green Flag Community Award for the quality of work they do on behalf of the local community.

Address Pentregethin Road, Swansea, SA5 4BA | **Getting there** Bus 25 or 43 to Cadlewood Road; on-street parking near reserve entrance | **Hours** Accessible 24 hours | **Tip** If you're inspired to attract more wildlife to your garden, B&M at Fforestfach has a garden centre where you might find what you're looking for.

15 Captain Cat
A beatific bronze

Captain Cat is a leading character in Dylan Thomas' radio drama *Under Milk Wood*. The play is set in the fictional village of Llareggub – 'bugger all' spelt backwards. Despite Dylan Thomas stating that Llareggub is based on Laugharne, where he lived for a while, this remains in dispute. Some think it is New Quay on the west coast of Wales, others that it was Llansteffan or Ferryside, both near Laugharne.

Wherever Llareggub may be, listeners are taken on a journey through the residents' dreams as dawn breaks and the village awakens. The journey continues as the day unfolds, finally returning to their dreams at the end of the day. The blind Captain Cat sits in his window, listening to the comings and goings of the village, and acts as a third narrator.

One of his roles in the play is to wake the villagers with his 'loud get-out-of-bed bell', which we can see him ringing here. Look closely at the statue. The details that the sculptor Robert Thomas included are exquisite. Captain Cat's face is a picture of total bliss, as though he is remembering his time as a sailor – when he could still see clearly and his true love, Rosie, was still alive. The buttons of his coat sport the letters I, L, Y, R, and P: 'I Love You, Rosie Probert'. The statue has stood on this spot since St David's Day in 1990 and will undoubtedly provide an enduring commemoration of Dylan Thomas' work.

The play was first sent to the publisher with the name *Llareggub*, but it was felt that such a title would not attract American audiences. Therefore, for commercial reasons, the play was renamed *Under Milk Wood*. Sadly, Dylan Thomas did not live to hear the play's first radio broadcast on the BBC in January 1954, narrated by his friend Richard Burton and Richard Bebb, with Captain Cat's voice provided by Hugh Griffith. Since then, it has also been performed as a film and on television.

Address Maritime Quarter, Swansea, SA1 1RT | Getting there Train to Swansea, then a 21-minute walk; bus 7 to Ferrara Square, or several to Sainsbury's Quay Parade; nearest parking at St David's multi storey | Hours Accessible 24 hours | Tip For a statue of Dylan Thomas himself, cross the marina and turn left to the square in front of the Dylan Thomas Theatre.

16 Caribbean Flamingos
In the pink

Watching the Caribbean flamingos at Llanelli Wetland Centre, it is easy to see how Lewis Carroll imagined using them as croquet mallets in *Alice in Wonderland*. As they walk with their heads in the water, siphoning food through their beaks, it seems perfectly feasible to pop one under your armpit, tuck its legs out of the way and swing the head towards a croquet ball. The bird might not be too impressed, though, just as they weren't impressed in the book.

On entering the shed where the birds hang out inside, the sound and movement are as remarkable as the coral pink. Some birds stand still, swinging their bodies from side to side as they feed in a circle around their feet. Others strut around, making a mournful noise somewhere between a honk and a quack, and others stand stationary with their necks stretched to their full height, turning their heads jerkily from side to side.

These are impressive birds. They fly with their necks and legs stretched straight, like an arrow with a body-shaped bulge in the middle, supported by wings with a span of up to 1.5 metres. They can fly as far as 600 kilometres (370 miles) in a night, at speeds of around 50 kilometres (30 miles) per hour. Flamingos are sociable birds that live in colonies, as here, and look after their chicks in shared crèches.

They are also incredible engineers. They build their nests on piles of mud. During hot weather, the nest is cooled by a slight updraft and capillary action pulling water up from below. During wet weather, the nest provides some protection against rising water.

Flamingos are only one of an impressive variety of birds found at Llanelli Wetland Centre. Around 60,000 birds overwinter here, and it has the only colony of black-headed gulls in South Wales. The pools also provide a habitat for other wildlife, such as otters and water voles.

Address WWT Llanelli Wetland Centre, Llwynhendy, Llanelli, SA14 9SH,
+44 (0)1554 741087, www.wwt.org.uk/wetland-centres/llanelli, info.llanelli@wwt.org.uk |
Getting there Bus 111 or L7 to The Joiners, Llwynhendy, then a 25-minute walk;
train to Llanelli, then a 40-minute walk; on-site parking | Hours Daily 9.30am–5pm |
Tip Blackpill Beach on Swansea Bay is a Site of Special Scientific Interest because
of its importance for overwintering birds. During winter, volunteers are on hand on
Sunday mornings to help visitors see the birds and learn about the annual migration
(www.swansea.gov.uk/blackpillSSSI).

17 Caswell Bay Surfability

Surf's up – for every body

Ask a seasoned surfer about the swell at Caswell Bay, and they are unlikely to be impressed. The waves are pretty regular but never spectacular, and generally smaller than those on other Gower beaches. However, this is precisely what makes Caswell Bay such an excellent and safe place for novices to experience surfing for the first time.

Not only that, but the beach has a Blue Flag for water quality and a Seaside Award that recognises how well it is managed. With parking near the sand, it is easy to access, including for people who use a wheelchair. A Changing Places toilet provides a hoist and changing bed for those who need some additional help. Standard wheelchairs quickly become bogged down in soft sand, so the council also provides a couple of floating beach wheelchairs for people to borrow. These enable access to the beach and the water for a wider range of people.

There are several surf schools on Caswell Bay, but Surfability stands out. First, it is a Community Interest Company designed to benefit the community rather than shareholders. Second, it is leading the way in the UK on accessible surfing. The coaches at Surfability will work with anyone, regardless of ability or disability, and they have designed specialist equipment to enable everyone to enjoy the sport. This includes the UK's first tandem surfboard, which has a seat so that people who cannot sit up unaided can still enjoy the thrill of riding the waves.

The coaches manage the Welsh Adaptive Surfing Team, which takes part in various international competitions. Surfability was not going to stop there, though: their Head Coach, Ben Clifford, has been involved in developing the International Surfing Association Adaptive Surf Instructor Qualification so that what they have learnt here in Caswell Bay, and the joy it brings, can be spread around the world.

Address The Canthed Centre, Caswell Bay, Swansea, SA3 3BS, +44 (0)1792 368482, www.surfabilityukcic.org, benedict@surfabilityukcic.org | Getting there Bus 2C or 3A to Caswell Bay; paid parking at Caswell Bay car park | Hours Check the website for booking information | Tip Experienced surfers consider the northern end of Rhossili Bay to offer the best waves in the area.

18 Central Police Station
'Ello, 'ello, 'ello!

Swansea's Central Police Station has two arresting features for urban explorers.

The first is a blue plaque to William Robert Grove, who lived in a house on this spot and invented the fuel cell in 1839. The name sounds technically advanced – and at the time, it was. Now, it has become an everyday item – the battery. This might seem like a small thing, but where would we be without it? No television remote controls, no wireless mice, no mobile phones, no cars, no space travel… The list is almost endless. William Grove was not just a ground-breaking scientist but also a talented lawyer who became Queen's Counsel and then a High Court Judge. The things you can achieve when you're not distracted by games on your mobile phone… If only the battery and electronic games had not been invented!

The second feature is rather more obvious – a tall fingerprint monolith in shiny steel stands at the road junction and gives an artistic breakdown of key dates in the history of policing. Did you know, for example, that the first British police were known as 'peelers' after Robert Peel MP, who set up the first police force? Or that Swansea continued to rely on local militias and night-watchmen, rather than a formal police force, until 1839? That fingerprints have been used to identify criminals since 1901?

Police telephone boxes were first placed at busy intersections in 1929. They were used by both police and the general public to contact the police station, and the light on the roof would flash to let the local bobby know to call in. It was not until Doctor Who came on the scene in 1963 that the flashing light indicated imminent time travel! The bottom section of the monolith provides us with an explanation of various acronyms, for example, BOB stands for Breach Of Bail, whereas BOP stands for Breach Of Peace – by dancing to loud music, perhaps?

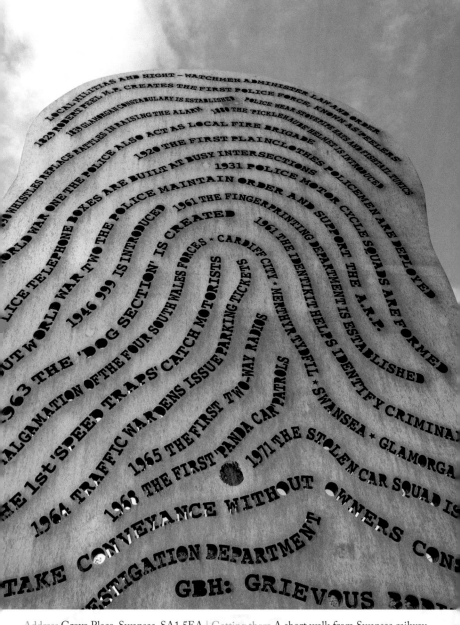

LOCAL MILITIAS AND NIGHT – WATCHMEN ADMINISTER LAW AND ORDER
1829 ROBERT PEEL M.P. CREATES THE FIRST POLICE FORCE, KNOWN AS 'PEELERS'
1839 GLAMORGAN CONSTABULARY IS ESTABLISHED · POLICE WEAR STOVEPIPE HATS AND TAILCOAT UNIFORMS
WHISTLES REPLACE RATTLES IN RAISING THE ALARM · 1880 THE 'PICKELHAUBE HELMET IS INTRODUCED
WORLD WAR ONE THE POLICE ALSO ACT AS LOCAL FIRE BRIGADE
1920 THE FIRST PLAINCLOTHES POLICEMEN ARE INTRODUCED
POLICE TELEPHONE BOXES ARE BUILT AT BUSY INTERSECTIONS
1931 POLICE MOTOR CYCLE SQUADS ARE FORMED
ABOUT WORLD WAR TWO THE POLICE MAINTAIN ORDER AND SUPPORT THE A.R.P.
1946 999 IS INTRODUCED · 1961 THE FINGERPRINTING DEPARTMENT IS ESTABLISHED
1963 THE 'DOG SECTION' IS CREATED · 1961 THE IDENTIKIT HELPS IDENTIFY CRIMINALS
AMALGAMATION OF THE FOUR SOUTH WALES FORCES · CARDIFF CITY · MERTHYR TYDFIL · SWANSEA · GLAMORGAN
THE 1st 'SPEED TRAPS' CATCH MOTORISTS
1964 TRAFFIC WARDENS ISSUE PARKING TICKETS
1965 THE FIRST TWO-WAY RADIOS
1968 THE FIRST 'PANDA CAR' PATROLS · 1971 THE STOLEN CAR SQUAD IS
TAKE CONVEYANCE WITHOUT OWNERS CONS
INVESTIGATION DEPARTMENT
GBH: GRIEVOUS BOD

Address Grove Place, Swansea, SA1 5EA | **Getting there** A short walk from Swansea railway station; bus 11, 12, 13 or 16 to Swansea Central Police Station, 16 to Belle Vue Way B, X13 Cymru Clipper to Kingsway D, or X11 Cymru Clipper to Kingsway E; nearest parking at Pell Street | **Hours** Viewable from the outside only | **Tip** An episode of series 14 of *Dr Who* is reported to have been filmed at Swansea University Bay Campus in January 2023.

19 Ceri Richards' Grave
A brush with greatness

Ceri Richards, born in the village of Dunvant near Swansea, ultimately became an artist of international repute. His journey started modestly, when he won a prize for art at his school in Gowerton. His education continued at Swansea School of Art and then the Royal College of Art in London, where he was exposed to a wide range of artistic styles and movements, which would later inform his diverse body of work.

His artwork spanned a broad church, from impressionism to surrealism and from painting to designing stained-glass windows. The influence of Picasso on his work can clearly be seen in his windows at Liverpool Metropolitan and Derby Cathedrals. In 1961, as a Welshman living in London, he would have been rightly proud of his achievements. During that year, he was awarded a gold medal at the National Eisteddfod, a celebration of the cultural heritage of Wales, as well as being honoured as a Commander of the Order of the British Empire (CBE) by Queen Elizabeth II.

However, 1962 might be seen as the year in which his career peaked. Representing Britain at the Venice Biennale was a significant milestone. This prestigious international art exhibition provided a platform for Richards to showcase his work to a global audience and consolidate his position as a leading figure in the art world. Winning the Einaudi Painting Prize at the Biennale was a testament to his exceptional talent and creativity, and it helped to establish his legacy as one of the most influential British artists of the 20th century.

Despite spending much of his life in England, Ceri Richards remained deeply connected to his Welsh roots. He frequently visited the Swansea area, drawing inspiration from the landscapes and communities of his homeland. He made his final journey back to the area to be interred with other members of his family in the village of his birth.

Address Ebenezer Congregational Chapel, Dunvant Square, Dunvant | Getting there Bus 116 to Post Office or 21, 22 or 116 to Dunvant Club; car to Dunvant car park | Hours Unrestricted | Tip The Clyne Cycle Path, shared with walkers, runs from Swansea Bay through Dunvant to Gowerton and Loughor.

20 Challenge Valley
No teddy bears' picnic

Venture into Challenge Valley expecting to stay clean, and you're in for a big, muddy surprise. The first few stages of the obstacle course could give you a false sense of security. An eight-foot fence with only a few centimetres of mud on the other side? Easy! A wibbly wobbly bridge over a muddy stream? No worries! If you're skilful – or lucky – you might even make it along the commando pole without landing in the mire, but you have no chance after that. Venture deeper into Challenge Valley to tackle ever-muddier obstacles that will test your mettle and appetite for adventure. You cannot crawl over muddy ground under a cargo net and stay clean. And the rope swing is almost certainly rigged, so reaching the other side is impossible without landing in the deep, gloopy mud. It's time to embrace the dirt and the challenge.

As you reach adulthood and take responsibility for your own washing, it's easy to fall into the habit of trying to keep your clothes clean. That's why this muddy obstacle course is so much fun. By its very nature, it releases the inner child. Embrace the liberation of getting dirty. Rediscover the joy of jumping into muck and flinging mud at your friends, and remember the days when muddiness equalled happiness.

Completing this obstacle course is not a race; it's set up to be safe and fun, whether you are competitive or not, and however fit you are. There is always an instructor on hand to tell you the best way to tackle an obstacle and keep you safe. They will not keep you clean, though. There is plenty of hot water to wash the mud off in the showers, but don't be surprised if you find some in odd places a few hours later, or if it's the end of the line for some of your clothes.

By visiting Challenge Valley, you are giving yourself permission to get muddy. Very muddy. And to have a mud fight. When did you last do that?

Address Clyne Farm Centre, Westport Avenue, Mayals, Swansea, SA3 5AR,
+44 (0)1792 403333, www.clynefarm.com | Getting there Bus 37 to Westport Avenue; free
parking on site | Hours Book in advance through the website | Tip The bouldering wall at
the Climbing Hangar on Swansea Enterprise Park offers an opportunity to climb with no
mud (www.theclimbinghangar.com).

21 __ Chicken Corner
Birds of a feather

Bird strikes cost the global airline industry over a billion US dollars a year in repairs and delays. Over 300 human lives and a similar number of aircraft have been lost when they have encountered flocks of birds in flight.

But what has this got to do with chickens or the King Arthur Hotel? One way to reduce the risk is to limit the number of birds living near airports. That has some effect, but it will never be enough on its own to reduce the risk to an acceptable level. We also need to design planes that will withstand bird strikes. Over time, required standards have improved, and critical components must be tested to ensure they can cope if they hit – or ingest – flocks of birds. To this end, chicken carcasses of varying sizes are shot into engines at 200 knots to emulate the birds a plane might strike during take-off or landing. The resultant impact on the engine is then measured against industry safety standards.

One night, 'Bomber Harris', a regular in the King Arthur Hotel, told his friends about how frozen chickens were shot at aircraft windscreens to test them. It seemed like such an outlandish tale that they were incredulous. The idea captured their imagination, and a little later, one of the locals brought a chicken into the bar – and started a trend. Now, the locals' corner is full of chickens. A rubber chicken hangs limply from the wall. A tin chicken dangles its legs from a shelf. Painted chickens peer through a layer of chicken wire, and a stained-glass chicken keeps its beady eye on proceedings. A cartoon of chickens piloting a plane flying towards a human cannonball finishes the scene with a flourish of humour.

Chicken Corner is still where the locals drink; now, they can always be sure of having some feathered friends for company and fond memories of Bomber Harris, even when the bar is otherwise empty.

Address King Arthur Hotel, Reynoldston, Swansea, SA3 1AD, +44 (0)1792 390775, www.kingarthurhotel.co.uk, info@kingarthurhotel.co.uk | Getting there Bus 115, 118 or 119 to King Arthur Hotel; parking on site | Hours Daily 9–11am for breakfast, 10am–11pm for drinks, noon–9pm for food | Tip If you like to fly, Cambrian Flying Club is based at nearby Swansea Airport (www.cambrianflyingclub.co.uk).

22 Cinema & Co
The only independent cinema in Swansea

How many cinemas do you know where customers lounge on comfy sofas and drink wine while watching a film? Everything about Cinema & Co is unusual, from the moment you step inside the door into the small, quirky coffee shop. Some of the seating is from Portmeirion's theatre, and the sofa is from a record shop in Surrey. Battered old suitcases on shelves house pot plants and dried flowers. Tea and coffee are available, but so are tequila, wine and whisky – the alcoholic drinks available only to cinema-goers.

Nicholas Cage looks down on the customers from a cage on the wall. The cushion on which his likeness is printed used to be on one of the café's sofas until, one day, it was stolen by a passerby. After an internet hunt for the perpetrator, it was apologetically returned. It is now caged for its own safety.

Customers here help to choose the films that are shown, which might explain the unusual mix of old and new, mainstream and indie. Monthly singles nights provide the possibility of romance, enticing customers from all over South Wales. And private hires range from romantic couples to groups of friends. The cinema also doubles as an art gallery and space for community events like clothes swaps.

News of the cinema has spread so far that even the local wildlife has been known to try to get in. First, a squirrel paid a fleeting visit. Then, a Muntjac deer ran into the café and tried to jump into the sink before darting around the room, looking for the exit.

In an age where streaming services and multiplex cinemas dominate the entertainment landscape, Cinema & Co is a testament to the power of community and the enduring magic of the silver screen. By involving customers in the selection of films and hosting a variety of events, this independent cinema has created a space in the centre of the city where people with shared interests can come together.

Address 17 Castle Street, Swansea, SA1 1JF, +44 (0)7305 908260, www.cinemaco.co.uk, info@cinemaco.co.uk | **Getting there** City centre location – several bus stops nearby | **Hours** See website for current information on visiting | **Tip** The Taliesin Arts Centre hosts the WOW Film Festival, showcasing films from Asia, Africa and Latin America, every March (Swansea University Singleton Campus, www.wowfilmfestival.com).

23 Clydach Aqueduct
From industry to amenity

Swansea Canal was built at the end of the 18th century to provide water and transport to the flourishing industries in the Swansea Valley. Coal was carried down to the port at Swansea and copper ore was transported up the valley to smelters. The canal was 25 kilometres long, with 5 aqueducts and 36 locks. It must have been a slow journey, but canal barges could carry massive quantities of materials compared to road vehicles, making it the best means of transport until the advent of rail.

As Swansea's industry declined and alternative means of transport were developed, the canal also declined. A century after the waterway opened, trade stopped along the higher sections, but the lower section to Clydach remained open until 1931. By the early years of the 21st century, no one was using the canal for transportation, and only one manufacturer still used it for water supply. In 2022, that company introduced a closed-loop cooling water circuit. This means it no longer needs water from the canal or river, saving over four billion litres annually. The canal is now fully redundant, except as an amenity for people and a habitat for wildlife.

The aqueduct carries the canal water over the Lower Clydach just before the river joins the Tawe. Overflows on each side create a two-metre-high sheet waterfall, as the spare water is discharged into the river. From the aqueduct, the view opens out over the broad, meandering River Tawe.

Although much of the canal has been infilled, short lengths remain open; this stretch is about 3.5 kilometres long. A path runs down the side, making it a perfect place to walk or cycle in the cool shade of the trees, with reflections of the sky and sounds of the waterfowl who have made this their home. At the end of the canal, pick up the path along the river, then hop back to the canal at Pontardawe for a few more kilometres of peaceful amble.

Address Accessed from Clydach High Street, SA6 | Getting there Several buses go to Three Compasses; on-street parking in the village | Hours Accessible 24 hours | Tip If you like your falls old fashioned, head to The Overdraft cocktail bar at 41 High Street, a little east of the aqueduct.

24 Colliery Winch
Rewinding time

The 1878 Ordnance Survey 25-inch map shows a working colliery at this site. The presence of this twin-cylindered horizontal winding engine suggests that it was a drift mine, running diagonally down within the hill. Initially, children would have been employed to push the wagons of coal out of the mine. When it was made illegal to employ young children underground, mining companies needed to become more inventive about how to transport coal to the surface. Winding engines, also known as winches, provided an alternative option to pull the wagons of coal out. This winch was designed by John Wild and Company of Oldham in 1891 and installed around 1912.

John Wild also devised a horizontal boring machine, which would have been far more productive – and humane – than a man chipping away at the coal face with a pick. One of these may also be rusting somewhere deep within the mine. It is likely that a man loaded coal into wagons that were then winched out by a woman. Women were popular mine employees because their wages were only half that of men. However, women were banned from working in mines from 1843, so many took jobs on the surface instead. Initially, this ban was to protect women from exploitation. It was repealed in 1990 in a different world, where mines were safer (although still not totally safe), and banning half the population from certain professions to protect them from exploitation was not seen as the ideal option.

Clyne Valley is now a mixed woodland and wildlife haven. When the winch was in use, it was a total contrast: a noisy, smelly, industrial landscape full of coal mines, clay pits, quarries, forges, brickworks and people labouring hard to earn a crust. Now, the main activities here are quiet: cycling along the disused railway line, angling in the old ponds and strolling through the woods with family and friends.

Address In Clyne Woods. Start at the Railway Inn, 553 Gower Road, Killay, Swansea, SA2 7DS | **Getting there** Bus 117, 118 or 119 to Railway Inn; limited parking at Railway Inn. Head downhill on the cycle path. Take the first obvious right after the turning to the brickworks on the left. Then take the second path on the right, and follow this until you reach the winch. | **Hours** Accessible 24 hours | **Tip** This cycle path is part of the National Cycle Network Route 4, which reaches from London to Fishguard. The 42 miles from Port Talbot to Kidwelly only has five miles on roads, all of which are quiet. The rest is on separate cycle paths like this.

25 Confucius Statue

Confucius said…

Confucius said, 'Education breeds confidence. Confidence breeds hope. Hope breeds peace.' Maybe that's why the Chinese government gave a statue of this ancient philosopher to Swansea University in 2009. Over 700 Chinese students attend the university, and another 2,000 Chinese people call Swansea home.

Confucius was a philosopher who lived 500 years before Christ. At the time, China was in turmoil and ruled by those who claimed birthright rather than wisdom or leadership skills. Confucius felt that the situation could be improved by drawing on over 1,000 years of Chinese culture. He used this to develop what has become known as Confucianism, to try to encourage a sense of personal virtue in his followers. He distilled his teachings into one thread, described by two concepts: chung and shu. Between them, they mean being true to yourself and humane to others. Many of Confucius' teachings remain relevant today, and many are similar to those found in the world's religions.

In the 16th and 17th centuries, Europeans started to translate the works of Confucius, but it was not until the 1960s that his philosophy flooded into popular culture. Perhaps it is appropriate, then, that this statue stands in a quadrangle amid uninspiring 1960s' and 1970s' university buildings. What is undoubtedly appropriate is that it overlooks a pond, the ideal place to step back from the busyness of the world and contemplate the meaning of life.

In seeing the statue, aesthetes might simply enjoy the curvaceous lines of the creamy stone. Students might investigate his teaching and consider which of his philosophies resonate with them. Lecturers might be reminded of the value of education and the importance of their role in developing their students' knowledge and confidence. And maybe Confucius was right – maybe that will all lead to a more hopeful and more peaceful future.

Address Swansea University, Singleton Park, Sketty, Swansea, SA2 8PP | **Getting there**
Several buses go to Swansea University Campus; park at Swansea University car park,
SA2 8PZ. The statue is in a quadrangle between the Vivian Tower and Glyndŵr Building |
Hours Unrestricted | **Tip** The Chinese in Wales Association (www.chineseinwales.org.uk)
has a mission to improve the lives of ethnic Chinese people in Wales. Its head office is
in Swansea.

26   Crwys Community Woodland

A wheely great place

A wheelchair-accessible boardwalk and path meanders through this delightful wood on the edge of the Gower Area of Outstanding Natural Beauty. A mix of young native trees shade the route and provide homes for wildlife. Follow the path through the woods, and you will find a pond right in the middle of the site. The pond fills from rainwater run-off from the village, so levels can change dramatically depending on weather conditions. As with many small ponds, it is liable to natural succession. During this process, plants grow, and mud accumulates until the pond becomes a bog and then, often, a woodland. But this pond has a job to do, so in 2022, it was re-dug, enlarged and deepened to ensure open water remains – for a while, at least.

The boardwalk takes you out over the water, so you can watch the wildlife up close. Through the summer months and into early winter, you have a chance of seeing dragonflies near the pond. Females either lay their eggs into plant material or directly into the water. It is not uncommon to see a female repeatedly dunking her rear end into a pond, leaving eggs behind. Some even dive right down into the water to lay their eggs. A few weeks or months later, the eggs hatch. The larvae then spend the next few months or years (depending on the species) prowling around the pond, voraciously eating and moulting.

Eventually, they are ready for their final larval moult. Look out for them climbing a stem to emerge from the water. They attach themselves firmly and slowly push out of their larval skin. The process is fascinating to watch, as the dragonfly seems to puff up into the spectacular adult we are all familiar with, ready for the cycle to begin again.

The woodland wildlife has been joined by some creative carvings; look out for a pair of frolicking badgers and an owl peeking out of its nest by the side of the path.

Address Tirmynydd Road, Three Crosses, Swansea, SA4 3PP, www.crwyscommunitywoodland.weebly.com | **Getting there** Bus 21 or 22 to Tirmynydd Farm; small car park on site | **Hours** Accessible 24 hours | **Tip** Head along the path from the far end of Caswell Bay car park for another woodland experience. This one has a round-house and is popular for picnics and barbecues.

27 _ Crymlyn Bog
From woodland to wetland

Peat is a fantastic preservative, as we see when ancient bodies are occasionally unearthed, more or less intact. Taking a core sample from peat can tell you much about the history of a place: preserved pollen gives an indication of plants that grew nearby, and pollution tells you about industrial activity. The cores from Crymlyn Bog tell us that the area was wooded from the 16th century to the early 18th century. There was a bit of agriculture but little industry nearby. From the mid-18th century to the early 19th century, the pollen that landed here was from birch and hazel, which indicates that it was still wooded. However, the pollen was joined by some pollutants, as you would expect from a heavily industrialised area such as Swansea. By the early 20th century, the area had been subjected to large-scale clearance of trees, and the pollutants associated with metal smelting were beginning to decline.

What we have now is the most extensive lowland fen in Wales. Around 10% of the site is wet woodland, and the nature reserve is managed to retain a variety of fenland habitats, including open water. This open water is crucial as the home to the fen raft spider, Britain's rarest and largest. Don't worry – they like the open water, so you are unlikely to bump into one as you traverse the boardwalks and paths that circle through the site. There are only three areas of the UK with fen raft spiders, all geographically separate. Too little is known about historical distribution to understand why, although there is probably a link with the general reduction in wetland sites. Four new sites have had the spider re-introduced in an attempt to protect it from extinction.

The bog is studded with striking royal ferns. The fronds can rise to over two metres, and the leaves turn copper in autumn; appropriate, perhaps, for a plant that thrives on the boundary of Copperopolis.

Address Dinam Road, Swansea, www.naturalresources.wales | Getting there Bus to Wern Terrace, Port Tennant, then a 16-minute walk; free parking on site during daylight hours. From Port Tennant, head up Tir John N Road, which becomes Dinam Road. Car park is one kilometre along on the right | Hours Open during daylight hours; car park locked at night | Tip At the north end of the site, there is a series of small concrete pads in the ground. These were used in World War II to anchor blimps, that forced enemy planes to fly above them, where they were more susceptible to anti-aircraft fire.

28 Cu Mumbles
The legend lives on

Copper is a soft, malleable metal that can be drawn into wires and has high thermal and electrical conductivity. Although already in use for thousands of years, it became indispensable in the age of electricity. Cu is copper's elementary symbol, and Cu Mumbles is named in homage to the area's history as the world's epicentre of copper production. Its design also reflects that history: the stairway has copper patterns in the wallcoverings, and the bar has a striking copper top stretching the width of the building. Cu Mumbles has also recognised the heritage of the structure by retaining the old arched roof.

The building was opened as the New Cinema in 1927, ready to usher in talking movies and the 'Golden Age of Hollywood'. It soon changed its name to the Regent Cinema and operated until 1939, when the Tivoli Picture Theatre opened nearby. This meant that when the Local Defence Volunteers (later known as the Home Guard) were established in 1940, the building was available to house the Mumbles branch's headquarters.

The impressive roster of bands that graced the stage during the venue's post-war years reads like a 'Who's Who' of rock and roll royalty. From the infectious grooves of Mungo Jerry, to Suzi Quatro, to the heavy metal thunder of Motorhead and Whitesnake, the building played host to an eclectic mix of musical talents.

The venue also has literary connections, as it was referenced in Dylan Thomas' short story 'Old Garbo' (as The Regal) and Kingsley Amis' short story 'Age Old Ceremony at Mumbles'.

Today, Cu Mumbles continues to be a vibrant hub for the arts, providing a platform for established and emerging artists. The monthly comedy night, often hosted by Britain's Got Talent semi-finalist Noel James, brings laughter to the town, while Swansea Jazz Club's diverse programming showcases the best of traditional and contemporary jazz.

Address 7 Castleton Walk Arcade, Newton Road, Mumbles, SA3 4AX, +44 (0)1792 363482, www.cumumbles.co.uk, info@cumumbles.co.uk | Getting there Several buses to Oystermouth Square; parking on the seafront | Hours See website for events listing | Tip Swansea International Jazz Festival takes place in June every year, at venues around the city (www.facebook.com/swanseajazzfestival).

29 Cwmdonkin Park

Where imagination runs free

Cwmdonkin Park is close to the poet Dylan Thomas' childhood home. So close that he talked about being able to hear the older children playing there after he had gone to bed. It is a place that he visited many times and that he reminisced about fondly. This is the place where he would run wild, climb trees and invent worlds; the place where his imagination ran free.

The park is also the setting for his poem 'The Hunchback in the Park'. A visit to the park will bring the poem to life. You can see the fountain, although the basin is a touch small for sailing boats in, and it no longer has either water or a cup chained to it. You can see the water in the pond, sitting still, as the hunchback did, and listen to the birds chirping in the trees. You can imagine the stand of bamboo and the sight of a lonely man being bullied by some and ignored by (or perhaps invisible to) others, simply because he has a physical disability.

This is a poem of loneliness and isolation, even in a place bustling with people. But it is also a poem that emphasises the strength of imagination. However isolated this man is, he still imagines a beautiful woman who visits him once the daily torment of the park is over. Perhaps this is also a poem about resilience and the ability to be mentally free, despite earthly constraints.

The park has been open since the 1870s. There was some disquiet at the time because it served wealthy people who didn't need it. This ultimately led to the creation of other parks in less-affluent parts of the town.

There are plenty of opportunities here to be with friends. You can play tennis, bowl or share a pot of tea in the café. You can sit with the bust of Dylan Thomas under the trees for some silent contemplation. And perhaps it would be a good place to look out for someone sitting on their own, and give them a few minutes of company.

Address Park Drive, Uplands, Swansea | Getting there Bus 15, 29 or 39 to Victoria Street, several to Uplands Shops, 5 to Notts Gardens; on-street parking nearby | Hours Accessible 24 hours | Tip For something a little stronger than a cup of tea, head to nearby Uplands, where there is a good variety of bars, pubs and restaurants.

30 Cwmllwyd Wood

Pips and pits

Between Swansea and Gowerton, a peaceful broadleaved woodland reveals stories of the city's industrial past. The trees were planted here around 100 years ago, but before that, the area was a hive of activity.

Swansea was once known as 'Copperopolis' because as much as 65% of the world's copper was smelted here. The copper ore was imported, first from Cornwall and then from around the world. The reason that Swansea was a good place for smelting was the presence of easily accessible coal seams in the area, plentiful water and a safe harbour for importing ore and exporting goods.

One primitive means of extracting coal was to dig a pit, a little like a well, and winch the coal out. The pit would be widened at the bottom into the coal seam, making a bell-shaped hole. Each hole was mined unpropped until it became unsafe or collapsed, and then another was dug nearby. The remains of 35 such 'bell pits' are visible in Cwmllwyd Wood, more evident in winter when the undergrowth has died back. This area was mined from the 17th century. However, as techniques became more efficient, allowing for more extensive exploration, bell pit mining declined. Near the coal workings, some apple trees grow amidst the other woodland trees, possibly the result of miners discarding the remains of their lunches.

The main species in the woodland is oak, with supporting roles taken by birch, holly, willow and rowan trees. There is a rich under-storey of ferns, ivy and bramble. Bluebells flood the woodland with colour and scent in May. Now, you can enjoy a circular walk through the woods, with boardwalks raised over the boggy patches and steps to help on the steeper slopes. An occasional bench provides the opportunity to rest and soak in the sights, sounds and smells of this wonderful woodland reserve, which come more alive, the longer you quietly wait.

Address 150 metres south of Nantllwyd Farm, Waunarlwydd Road, Waunarlwydd, Swansea, SA5 4RP | **Getting there** Bus 15 or 16 to Waunarlwydd Village Inn, then a nine-minute walk; space for one or two cars at side of forest track | **Hours** Accessible 24 hours | **Tip** For tree-lovers, St James Gardens in Sketty is a delight of mature exotic trees that were status symbols for Victorians.

31 Daniel James' Tomb
A pure heart

Not many people can make a living from poetry, and Daniel James was no exception to the rule. His first wife died young, leaving him with four young children to care for. Maybe that is why he quickly remarried, although his new wife, a widow, brought more children into the family – and that was before they started producing their own. With more than 10 children in his household, he had a lot of mouths to feed, and this was done primarily through hard, regularly paid work, first at a tinplate works, then down a coal mine.

He was taught how to write poetry by an elder at Mynyddbach Chapel, the church where his parents were married and he worshipped when he lived nearby – and where his gravestone now stands. Daniel James wrote under the pen name 'Dafydd Mynyddbach' and his bardic name 'Gwyrosydd'. His passion for writing led to the publication of three books of poetry. The second contained a poem called 'Calon Lân', which means 'A Pure Heart' and lyricises about how much finer a pure heart is than any amount of material wealth. He invited the composer John Hughes to set it to music, and the rest, as they say, is history.

'Calon Lân' became a popular hymn, important during the 1904–1905 Welsh Revival when over 100,000 people were baptised. Later, it became a rugby anthem, familiar to anyone who follows the sport. More recently, it has been taken up by Wales football fans and can be heard reverberating around the stands at any international match, helping to keep the language and spirit of Wales alive.

No one knows quite where 'Calon Lân' was written. Some say it was in a hotel bar that Daniel James frequented, where he was reputed to have written verse in exchange for alcoholic drinks. Most would agree that it doesn't matter; it is a hymn that the Welsh people have embraced and has brought the nation together, proving that a pure heart wins out any day.

Er Cof Am
ANN
ANNWYL BRIOD
DANIEL JAMES TREBOETH
YR HON A FU FARW RHAGFYR 24, 1887,
YN 38 MLWYDD OED.
WELE FEDD UN ANNWYL FUYN HEULWEN
DDIHALOG IW THEULU NI ROWD IW BEDDROD DU.
HEFYD
WILLIAM JAMES
EU MAB YN 20 MLWYDD OED.
HEFYD Y RHAGENWYD
DANIEL JAMES (GWYROSYDD)
YR HWN A BU FARW MAWRTH 16, 1920,
YN 73 MLWYDD OED.
CALON LAN YN LLAWN DIONONT
HEFYD MERCH YR UCHOD
MARY
A FU FARW MEHEFIN 28 1941,
YN 63 MLWYDD OED
FENDIGEDIGION FY NHAD ETIFEDDWCH
Y DEYRNAS A BARATOWYD I CHWI.

Address Mynyddbach Chapel, Tirdeunaw, Swansea, SA5 7HT | Getting there Bus 35, 36 or 43 Welcome Inn; parking on site | Hours Accessible 24 hours | Tip The Welcome Inn is the second oldest pub in Swansea and where Swansea Jack used to lie in front of the fire.

32 Dunvant Brickworks

Where orienteering meets industry

Brickworks abounded in the Swansea area in the late 18th and early 19th centuries, providing a valuable resource to support the growth of industry and housing in the area. Bricks are made by digging clay from the ground, mixing it with water to create a paste, forming it into a brick shape using a mould, drying it out, and finally firing it in a hot kiln to harden it and stop it from dissolving in the rain. The remnants of the Dunvant Brickworks are now deeply buried in woodland. However, some industrial remains can be spotted in the verdant growth. These include a few fragments of buildings and a pond that has formed in the hollow of the clay pit.

The site is now home to an orienteering course, so there are several choices of paths to follow when exploring. For some, orienteering is a competitive sport in which they navigate between checkpoints as quickly as possible. For others, it provides a fun challenge that helps them to develop and maintain their navigational and map-reading skills. Orienteering was first developed towards the end of the 19th century as a military training exercise for the Swedish army. A few years later, people from outside the armed forces adopted the sport and the first civilian competition was held in Norway. Following this, orienteering slowly gained in popularity within the Nordic countries, aided by the development of more reliable compasses. After World War II, it spread through Europe and North America, and the 1960s saw it become a truly international sport.

Specialist orienteering maps show the location of the control posts in Dunvant Brickworks. These have a red and white orienteering symbol on a plaque, with a number telling you which post it is and a letter to record as evidence of reaching the post. Dunvant Brickworks is one of a dozen permanent orienteering courses in the Swansea area.

Address Dunvant Car Park, SA2 7ST, www.swansea.gov.uk/orienteering | Getting there
Bus 116 to Post Office or 21, 22 or 116 to Dunvant Club; car to Dunvant car park | Hours
Unrestricted | Tip If orienteering sounds like fun, Swansea Bay Orienteering Club organises
regular events in the area (www.sboc.org.uk).

33__Dylan Thomas' Birthplace
From plagiarism to poetry

When people think of Dylan Thomas' home, many think of the boat-house and writing shed in Laugharne. In fact, most of his published work was written while he lived at 5 Cwmdonkin Drive, now run as a small museum. This was his birthplace and childhood home, where he lived until he was in his 20s.

Dylan's father was a working-class boy who won a scholarship to Aberystwyth University and graduated with a first-class honours degree in English. He became a teacher and moved up the social ladder to the point where the family lived in a favoured residential area of Swansea and employed servants.

This was the world that Dylan Thomas was born into. That said, his room in the house was a tiny single room. The small bed, desk and bookshelf fill all the available space. A couple of hooks on the wall provided for hanging clothes. One corner of the room has been lost to the boiler cupboard, the sound of which he used to complain about. His father's study was more spacious. It was here that Dylan's father would read Shakespeare to him from an early age. Determined to impress him, Dylan managed to get a poem published in the *Western Mail* newspaper when he was just 12. His father was rightly proud of his son's achievement. However, he might not have been quite so proud when it came to light many years later that the poem had been plagiarised from a copy of *Boy's Own* paper.

Nevertheless, Dylan Thomas wrote many original works based on his experience of life growing up in Swansea, including the poem 'The Hunchback in the Park' and the short story 'Patricia, Edith and Arnold', both set in Cwmdonkin Park, a short walk from 5 Cwmdonkin Drive. The house itself has been restored as closely as possible to how it was when Dylan lived there, while remaining a habitable holiday rental space for those who would like to experience a slice of his life.

Address 5 Cwmdonkin Drive, Swansea, SA2 0RA, +44 (0)1792 472555, www.dylanthomasbirthplace.com, info@dylanthomasbirthplace.com | **Getting there** Bus 5 to Cwmdonkin Park, several to Uplands Shops; limited on-street parking nearby | **Hours** Viewable from outside 24 hours; book in advance for a tour | **Tip** Learn more about Dylan Thomas' life at the Dylan Thomas Centre in the Maritime Quarter (Somerset Place, SA1 1RR, www.dylanthomas.com).

34 E&R Harding Nature Reserve

Layers of time

The Elizabeth and Rowe Harding Nature Reserve is designated and protected as a Site of Special Scientific Interest. Unusually, this is not because of living nature, but animals that died millions of years ago. The limestone quarry providing the backdrop to this reserve was worked until the mid-1960s, leaving a rock face unique in Wales. The layers of limestone, which is made of the debris from sea-dwelling creatures, are interspersed with layers of soil, which is generated on land. This pattern tells us a lot about the frequent sea-level changes during the early Carboniferous period.

The growth of plants on the quarry face is being controlled to keep these layers visible, and a band of scrub has been left along the upper lip to stabilise the quarry face, reducing the risk of rock falls. The nature reserve is being managed as coppiced woodland with standards. This form of intensive management has been practised for thousands of years and creates a plentiful wood crop as well as a rich habitat for wildlife. Most trees are cut back to ground level every so often, while others are left to grow to their full height. This extends the life of the trees, and the occasional years of light and warmth reaching the woodland floor create perfect conditions for spring flowers to thrive.

The nature reserve is named after its former owners, who gifted it to the local Wildlife Trust. Rowe Harding was a Welsh International rugby player who grew up in the area and also played for local clubs. He retired at 28 to pursue a career in law, working his way up the ranks to become a County Court Judge in his 50s.

The reserve can be accessed from Ilston or a small parking area near a ford just north of the village. Please take care crossing the ford. When in the reserve, follow the path around to the right to reach the quarry face. It can be wet underfoot; wellies are recommended.

Address Just north of Ilston, Gower | Getting there Bus 119 to Ilston turn, then a 17-minute walk to the reserve; limited parking at entrance to reserve | Hours Accessible 24 hours | Tip There's a spectacular rock arch you can see through and walk over on Worm's Head at the far end of the Gower Peninsula, but only when the tide is low (park at National Trust, Rhossili).

35 Egypt Centre
Not your average lucky dip

When Henry Wellcome died in 1936, he left a challenge to the beneficiaries of his estate: he had collected more than a million objects that needed to be re-homed. In the early 1970s, Swansea University acquired 92 sealed tea chests from the collection. No-one knew what was inside.

Can you imagine the anticipation in the room as the first chest was opened? The first object unwrapped was an Egyptian antiquity. Thousands more followed, and the Egypt Centre at the university was born. From the bottom of one of the last chests, a heavy object about the size of a rugby ball was carefully lifted out. It was a head carved from stone. Less than 40 of these 'reserve heads' have ever been unearthed, all from tombs around Memphis and Giza. No-one knows what they represent or why they were placed in the tombs – one of the many mysteries of Ancient Egypt.

Opening the tea chests was not your average lucky dip, and this is not your average museum. In the House of Death, visitors can help eviscerate a mummy several times a day. In the House of Life, visitors can write their names in hieroglyphics and handle objects thousands of years old. And all of this can be done while dressed as an Ancient Egyptian! Knowledgeable volunteers are on hand to bring the exhibits to life or challenge you to a game of senet as played by King Tutankhamun.

One of the most popular exhibits in the House of Death is the coffin of Iwesenhesetmut (known as 'Izzy'). Izzy was a 'Lady Chantress' – a temple singer – and her coffin is typical of the time. It is glazed yellow with beautiful paintings along the side depicting her journey to the afterlife and the roles of the different gods in the process. The exhibits in the House of Life are more representative of everyday life, including bead necklaces, ceramic storage pots of varying sizes and wooden headrests that were used instead of pillows.

Address Museum of Egyptian Antiquities, Swansea University, Singleton Park, Swansea, SA2 8PP, +44 (0)1792 295960, www.egypt.swan.ac.uk | **Getting there** Buses (various) to Swansea University; paid parking at entrance to campus, SA2 8PZ | **Hours** Tue–Sat 10am–4pm | **Tip** Head north-east from the Egypt Centre and you will soon arrive at Singleton Abbey, the mansion that was once the home of industrialist John Vivian.

36   Elysium Gallery
Paradise found?

What comes to mind if you close your eyes and conjure up an image of 'Elysium'? A serene natural paradise, where trees sway gently in the breeze, together offering respite from the heat of the sun, or where a lake reflects forests leading up to snow-covered peaks and a cerulean sky? If so, prepare for a shock when you first push through the doors into this Elysium. An alternative interpretation of Elysium is a world of abundance. In this Elysium, there is no need for toil. Everyone has time to engage in whatever artistic pursuits they take most pleasure from. Step into this groovy, psychedelic bar and give yourself the gift of time. Time to lose yourself to the beat of live music, savour the words of poets, laugh at life with the stand-up comedians, or wonder at the creativity of cabaret. Give yourself time to engage in easy conversation while working on your latest craft project, or concentrate on learning the art of life drawing. Lose track of time as you wander through the galleries that showcase the work of emerging local artists, sit in quiet contemplation with a soothing drink or watch artist conversations online.

And if all of that motivates you to create art as well as consuming it, let Elysium inspire you with its art and craft workshops, where you can learn a new skill or improve on an existing one, either onsite or in the community. If you want to take things a step further, you can hire studio space where you can spend as much time as you like honing your expertise and collaborating with other artists in your creative journey.

This Elysium is not just a place; it is a state of mind, a celebration of creativity and a sanctuary for artistic souls, whether creators, consumers or both. This non-profit has a vision to make the inspiration and artistic energy of Elysium spill over to form an essential thread in the tapestry of city life. Does that sound like your kind of paradise?

Address 210 High Street, Swansea, SA1 1PE, +44 (0)1792 648178, www.elysiumgallery.com, info@elysiumgallery.com | Getting there A short walk from Swansea railway station; several buses stop along the High Street; nearest parking in High Street car park | Hours Wed–Sat 11am–9pm | Tip Three doors further up the road, Swansea Community Workshops also offers crafting opportunities (www.sccw.org.uk).

37 The Environment Centre
Creating a brighter future

Swansea Environment Centre's literature suggests that they help us to 'imagine the future we want'. They go much further than that – they help to create a greener future through public awareness and engagement. Although the Environment Centre is in a historic building in a Conservation Area, it has had some distinctive features added. Planters made from recycled plastic, containing edible herbs and fruit, line the edge of the pavement. The guttering downpipe feeds into a small, raised pond that overflows into containers on each side, full of damp-loving plants. Not only does this provide a mini habitat for wildlife, but it also slows down the rain from the roof so that it does not flow into the drains at the same time as the rest of the rain. One downpipe might not make much difference. However, if similar mini wetlands were created on many downpipes, it could help alleviate flooding, as well as improving the look and feel of the streetscape.

That theory of many small steps ultimately making a significant difference permeates everything the Environment Centre does. It works with community groups to reduce their carbon footprint and with individuals to help them become climate leaders. It provides a refill shop to reduce the amount of plastic packaging used and recycling facilities for a weird and wonderful assortment of goods that would otherwise end up in landfill. Its energy awareness hub provides advice about reducing bills, increasing the use of renewable energy, and accessing grants and benefits if needed. The centre holds a monthly repair café, where locals can take broken goods they can't repair themselves, to be given a new lease of life. These activities bring the 'reduce, reuse, recycle' mantra to life.

Aware that all positive impacts need to be magnified to be effective, the centre is also part of several networks including Swansea CAN (Climate Action Network).

Address Pier Street, Swansea, SA1 1RY, +44 (0)1792 480200, www.environmentcentre.org.uk, info@environmentcentre.org.uk | **Getting there** Bus 7 to Burrows Place; several car parks nearby | **Hours** Shop and café Tue–Fri 10am–4pm, Sat 10am–2pm | **Tip** The Environment Centre is one of several litter-picking hubs in the area where you can borrow equipment. Most others are in libraries (keepwalestidy.cymru/caru-cymru/litter-picking-hubs).

38 Felinfoel Baptismal Pool
A sober celebration

How must it have felt to be immersed in the icy waters of the Lliedi River, fully dressed and with everyone you know looking on? Invigorating? Liberating? Life-affirming? The first baptism in Felinfoel is thought to have occurred before the British Civil Wars of 1642–1651. Britain briefly became a republic after the Parliamentarians won, but it wasn't long before the crown was restored and, with it, religious intolerance. Baptists who valued their lives had to worship in secret, so it is likely that no-one was baptised in public here for a while. Towards the end of the 17th century, an Act of Religious Tolerance was passed. Nonconformists were again allowed to worship openly, and at the beginning of the 18th century, the first Baptist chapel was built in Felinfoel. Initially, baptisms are likely to have taken place in the village millpond, but during the same century, a dam was built to hold back the waters of the Lliedi River and create a purpose-built baptismal pool.

During the Welsh Revival of 1904–1905, over 100,000 people across the country were converted. Baptism was seen as a way to cleanse their sins and gain God's forgiveness for all their misdemeanours. This was a busy time for the baptismal pool, and on one occasion, over 100 baptisms took place in just one day. Most of the village must have been at the party after that, although with the revival in Baptism came a reduction in the consumption of alcohol, so it was probably a relatively sober affair.

Brambles now reach across the steps to the water, although there was a baptism here as recently as 2014. During the ceremony, the man being baptised wore a rugby shirt, and the minister used football shirts to illustrate the importance of baptism and putting Jesus at the centre of your life. It makes you wonder what those first Baptists would have made of that degree of informality! Imagine how cold that must have been for the minister!

Address Near the Royal Oak Inn, Felinfoel, Llanelli, SA14 8LA | Getting there A 50-minute walk from Llanelli railway station; bus 128 or L2 to Royal Oak; on-street parking nearby | Hours Accessible 24 hours | Tip Head uphill for a few metres to Felinfoel Park.

39 Felinfoel Brewery
A canny business

In this area, the red dragon of Felinfoel Brewery is ubiquitous. How did such a large brewery get to be based in a small village outside the industrial town of Llanelli? It all started with one of the factory owners who lived in Felinfoel. Back in the 1830s, he decided to diversify and bought the coaching inn near his home. As usual at the time, the pub brewed its own beer, which soon became popular enough to be sold in other pubs. As demand grew, the pub no longer had the space it needed for brewing. The obvious answer? The owner built a brewery in the grounds of his house, which was just over the road and conveniently had the Lliedi River flowing through it.

The family continued to grow the business, but all was nearly lost in 1908 when they discovered a coal seam running beneath the brewery. Llanelli's wealth was built on the use and export of coal, and the family had some mining interests in their business portfolio. It was tempting to mine this seam, too, but ultimately, they decided to ignore the coal and keep the brewery running instead, alongside the mineral water and ginger beer business that also operated from the site.

Meanwhile, the tinplate industry was struggling. Most of the tinplate produced in Llanelli was exported to the United States, and changes to import tariffs had significantly reduced demand. The family saw an opportunity to use the tinplate for canning beer, which would benefit both businesses. The trouble was, the beer in cans tasted tinny. After much trial and error, Felinfoel Brewery was the first company in the world to successfully can unpasteurised beer. The original cans were tapered at the top to resemble a bottle so the bottling line would not have to be replaced. The brewery – and its canning process – have been modernised since then. However, it still stands on the same site, straddling the River Lliedi in Felinfoel.

Address Farmers Row, Felinfoel, Llanelli, SA14 8LB, +44 (0)1554 773357,
www.felinfoel.com, brewery@felinfoel.com | Getting there A 50-minute walk from Llanelli
railway station; bus 128 to Felinfoel Brewery; on-street parking nearby | Hours Viewable
from the outside only | Tip To sup a pint yourself, there are several pubs in Felinfoel,
including the Royal Oak Inn, about 50 metres north of the brewery.

40 Fendrod Lake

From flooding to fitness

When we erect buildings and hard landscaping, rain flows off them far faster than it does when seeping through the ground. This causes rivers to rise quickly and flooding to occur downstream. So, when Swansea Enterprise Park was built, Fendrod Lake was created to take that rainwater and slow its descent through the city. But Fendrod Lake is far more than just a flood remediation area surrounded by large sheds and businesses. It has also become a wonderful amenity for the area. Its proximity to people makes it the ideal location for outdoor pursuits and walking dogs, and water-loving wildlife flocks to it.

The lake covers over five hectares (13 acres). It is almost exactly one mile round, which is very useful for runners and walkers who want to measure either distance or speed. On one side of the lake is an outdoor gym with a mixture of equipment for warming up, cardio work and strength training. A free gym with fantastic views, your own choice of music piped directly into your ears and natural air conditioning – what's not to like?

If you prefer your hobbies to be somewhat less energetic, then the Brynmill and District Angling Club has the answer. They manage a plentiful supply of fishing pontoons, some of which are wheelchair accessible. The lake is well stocked with several species of fish, including carp and bream. When not being used by anglers, the pontoons are a great way to get down to the water for a bit of wildlife spotting, pond-dipping, or simply admiring the view.

The lake is fringed with water lilies, and orchids grow on the banks. Trees shade some of the path around the lake, and other areas are more open. Many birds visit or live on the lake, including large flocks of swans and ducks, all clamouring for food. Please remember that bread is bad for them; if you want to feed them, use a food mix specifically designed for waterfowl.

Address Valley Way, Llansamet, SA6 8RN | Getting there Bus 31, 33 or 34 to Castle Court; parking on site | Hours Accessible 24 hours | Tip If you enjoy seeing the birds at Fendrod Lake, you might also enjoy a visit to Blackpill Beach, which is a Site of Special Scientific Interest thanks to the number of overwintering birds it hosts.

41 Fishing Fleet

Changing tides – from abundance to alarm

Since the area was first settled, the people of Swansea have always fished. However, it was not until a large wharf, fish market and ice factory were built on the bank of the River Tawe in 1889 that a deep-sea fishing industry could operate from the town. The ice was used to keep fish fresh at the market, and as much as 60 tonnes of it was loaded into ships to enable them to tackle longer voyages into deeper water.

As a result of this development, the Castle Steam Trawler Company moved from Milford Haven to Swansea in 1904, bringing boats and jobs with it. The existing wharf proved inadequate, so a new one was built in the South Dock basin, where the marina is now. This was expanded in 1919, allowing a fleet of around 40 deep-sea fishing vessels to operate from the town. By 1930, the haul was as much as 15,000 tonnes, but it soon began to decline. By 1970, the catch was only 279 tonnes.

Now, just a small fleet of around 30 boats operates from the marina, 90 per cent of which are less than 10 metres long. Several factors have created a crisis for the industry in recent years. Brexit slashed the EU export market. Stronger legislation has increased costs. Catch limits are set so high that fish stocks around the UK are rapidly declining. And climate change is making it harder for fish populations to thrive, with many juvenile cod, for example, not surviving to adulthood. Only half of the top 10 species for the UK fishing industry are fished sustainably and have healthy populations. The other five now have critically low numbers. This devastation of the oceans is also causing significant social and financial hardship as fishing communities like Swansea are hit by a ruinous drop in catches.

For now, fishing vessels can still be seen loading and unloading on the quayside, but that might not remain the case for much longer. Enjoy it while you can.

Address Pilot House Wharf, Swansea, SA1 1UN | Getting there Bus 7 to Swansea Marina; nearest car park Swansea Point | Hours Unrestricted | Tip El Pescador restaurant on Meridian Wharf won Restaurant Guru's Best Seafood Restaurant in Swansea award in 2023.

42 The Flintstones Bus

Raising the roof

L78 looks like a single-decker version of a classic London double-decker because that is precisely what it is. During the 1950s, buses started to be built with the engine underneath the floor, which raised the roof height. In most places, this was fine, but not on one particular route in the New Dock area of Llanelli. Here, some of the railway bridges only had a clearance of nine feet (2.74 metres). The new single-decker buses could not fit underneath them.

To resolve this issue, eight new buses were commissioned specially for this route. They were built with a single deck on top of the chassis and engine of a double-decker. This created a bus that was eight feet and 10 inches high (2.69 metres) and was just low enough to clear the bridges. However, the suspension was designed to hold a far heavier deck, so it was rather unforgiving. One of the trustees at the Swansea Bus Museum and Transport Heritage Centre used to ride on this bus. It was affectionately known as the 'Flintstones Bus' because it felt like it had stone wheels.

The first two were built in 1959. Six more, including L78, were introduced into the fleet in 1963. After nine years, L78 was withdrawn from service in Llanelli and taken first to Northumberland, then to West Yorkshire, before being retired. After being passed around a few times, the Swansea Bus Museum acquired it in 2011 and started a complete restoration programme. It is the last of the eight to survive. The bus is once again operational and travels back to its roots every September to be admired during the Llanelli Vintage Festival.

Swansea Bus Museum has a fine collection of vintage buses, lovingly looked after by a team of volunteers. Their collection extends to vintage cars, emergency vehicles, and even a Sinclair C5. The museum also sometimes offers the opportunity to drive one of its buses, as well as hiring them out for events.

Address Swansea Bus Museum and Transport Heritage Centre, 2 Viking Way, Winch Wen, Swansea, SA1 7DA, +44 (0)1792 732832, www.swtpg.org.uk, secretary@sbm.wales | Getting there Bus 45 to Colliers' Arms; on-site parking | Hours Sat 11am–3pm, events and groups by appointment | Tip Every June, the city centre is filled with hundreds of classic cars and thousands of visitors for the Swansea Classic Vehicle Show (www.swanseaclassicvehicle.show).

43 Formal Cascades
Grand designs

When most people add a water feature to their garden, it might be a small pond or fountain. The Mackworths of Gnoll House had grander ambitions. Early in the 18th century, they started creating a garden around the house. The formal elements included a terrace, parterres – low hedges around floral planting creating an elaborate pattern – and an avenue of sweet chestnut trees. The more naturalistic elements included three ponds, one of which forms the centrepiece of the country park today. This lake-sized pond was stocked with carp, giving the family access to fresh fish for their table.

Not finished yet, they decided to add two sets of cascades – one formal and one informal. The formal one cascades water down a series of steps in a straight line from the top of the woods to the fish pond at the bottom. Stone sets with uneven surfaces were added to make the water more lively, adding movement and sound. Although built for reasons of status and aesthetics, the cascades would have had the added benefit of aerating the water in the pond, ensuring there was enough oxygen for the fish.

And how was all this paid for? The land was initially gifted to the Earl of Pembroke by Elizabeth I, and the first house was then bought by a salt magnate. The Mackworths made their fortune by making products from the brass and iron manufactured a few miles away in Swansea.

As a wealthy family who wished to maintain their social status, the Mackworths seem to have taken their food and drink seriously. Although the house fell into disrepair and was demolished in the mid-20th century, the cellars remain, as does some of the documentation relating to the house. An inventory from 1763 lists more than 475 bottles of wine, spirits, beer and cider in the cellar. A later inventory gives the number at over 800. That would have kept them going for a party or two!

Address Gnoll Estate Country Park, Fairyland, Neath, SA11 3BS, +44 (0)1639 635808, www.gnollestatecountrypark.co.uk, contactus@npt.gov.uk | **Getting there** Bus 153 from Neath to Fairyland; parking on site | **Hours** Daily 8am–5pm (winter), 8am–7pm (summer) | **Tip** As you explore what is now Gnoll Estate Country Park, you might stumble upon other follies hidden away in the woods, including a 'temple' and a grotto. Newer attractions include an adventure playground for children and a café by the fish pond.

44 Fort Crox

See You Later, Alligator

Have you ever wondered about the best way to wrestle a crocodile? Apparently, the key is to hold its jaws shut – preferably before any part of you is between them. Crocodiles have weak jaw-opening muscles, so you should be able to keep its teeth together. On the other hand, they have exceptionally strong jaw-closing muscles, so you won't be able to force its mouth open once it's shut. Please do not take this as an invitation to test the theory!

Fort Crox is home to a group of spectacled caimans, which can grow to about 2.4 metres long in their native habitat, from southern Mexico down to Argentina. There are some breeding populations in the United States, too, where they are invasive and at risk of out-competing native alligators.

Some of the animals here in Plantasia are under threat in the wild. In particular, the Egyptian tortoises are critically endangered on the International Union for the Conservation of Nature's red list, meaning they are very close to extinction in the wild. The tortoises here were rescued from being smuggled for the pet trade and are now part of a breeding programme to build up a stock for re-introduction into the wild. These are small tortoises that fit into the palm of a hand, with tiny babies that are only the size of a grape when they hatch. They love being stroked, and there's no need for keepers to worry about losing any limbs while handling these little herbivores. That's probably what makes them so attractive for the illegal pet trade – please take care to acquire pets responsibly.

While the tortoises graze continuously, the caimans do not need to eat very often – no more than three times a week. The offer of food draws them out from hiding, so to guarantee seeing them, you can arrange with the zoo to be the one serving their dinner – the only crocodile-feeding experience in Wales.

Address Plantasia Tropical Zoo, Parc Tawe, Swansea, SA1 2AL, +44 (0)1792 474555, www.plantasiaswansea.co.uk, plantasia@parkwood-leisure.co.uk | Getting there A 10-minute walk from Swansea railway station; several buses go to Sainsbury's Quay Parade; parking on site | Hours Daily 10am–5pm | Tip Playzone in Llansamlet offers an opportunity for children to let off some steam. The slides, climbing frames and ball pits are open to adults twice a month (www.theplayzone.co.uk).

45 __ Gower Brewery Tap
Finding Gold

Gower Gold is possibly the best-known beer in the area, loved by locals and visitors alike. The Gower Brewery claims to be inspired by the Area of Outstanding Natural Beauty that it operates in – the sandy beaches, rugged coves and open moorland of the Gower Peninsula and the sparkling waters of the Bristol Channel, Atlantic Ocean, Loughor Estuary and Carmarthen Bay.

The reality of the brewery is somewhat different. It operates from a shed on a small industrial estate within this beautiful landscape. The brewers undoubtedly have stunning views on their commute, but not from the brewery itself. However, if you stop for a taster in their tap room, they might argue that the beer itself will transport you to the sandy surfing beaches, clifftops overlooking the sea or Atlantic salt meadows studded with sheep.

The owners of the brewery completed their first brew (Brew1) at 4pm on 11 November, 2011. That's 11/11/11, whichever way round you write your dates. Tidy! (As the locals would say.) Brew1 was soon joined by Gower Gold, Gower Power and Lighthouse Lager (named after Whiteford Point). Since then, the brewery has gone from strength to strength, winning awards left, right and centre. In 2017, they even managed to turn a mistake into a success. One batch of Gower Gold went wrong during the brewing process. Rather than destroying it, the team decided to taste it. It did not taste like Gower Gold, but it did taste good. The brewery had discovered a new recipe, which they named after the remains of the *Helvetia* on Rhossili beach. The popular 'Shipwreck' beer was born.

The tap bar itself is modern, cosy and stylish, and you can also book the brewery's warehouse as an events space for parties, shows or festivals, accommodating up to 499 people. What better place to taste all the beers, freshly off the production line?

Address Unit 25, Crofty Industrial Estate, Penclawdd, Gower, SA4 3RS,
+44 (0)1792 850681, www.gowerbrewery.com, info@gowerbrewery.com | Getting there
Bus 116 to Hermon; car park on site | Hours See website for seasonal hours | Tip The wreck
of the *Helvetia* can be seen in the sands of Rhossili Bay at low tide, close to Rhossili village.

46 Gower Castaway Adventure

Into the wild

The adventure starts with a high-speed exploration of the Gower coastline, during which you are likely to see seals and seabirds, as well as the spectacular cliffs and caves of the Gower Peninsula from sea level. You might see a pod of porpoises or dolphins if you are lucky. Just as you are getting comfortable, the boat will land you in a remote location and depart.

Experienced instructors from Dryad Bushcraft will lead you through the key bushcraft skills you need to make your time with them comfortable – or at least less uncomfortable. They will teach you to hold a knife safely so you don't lose a finger and use an axe without losing a foot. Now that's done, you can cut some wood for the fire. You will also learn to make string from nettles and identify plants to forage for the larder. Don't worry, there's always plenty of food – you won't go hungry if you don't gather as much as you need.

Next up is learning to make fire with a bow. No matches or firestick. Just a piece of wood, a stick, a length of string, a shell and a bushcraft knife. Learning these new skills is utterly engrossing and thoroughly enjoyable in the woodland surroundings of the Dryad Bushcraft camp. That said, prepare for some frustration as you first try to make fire. The instructors make it look easy – they have done it a thousand times before – but it is skilled and hard work, and you are unlikely to succeed the first time you try. Imagine the sense of achievement when you do eventually see a glow, then a lick of fire. The next step is to think about somewhere to sleep. What sort of shelter can you make, and how can you best stay warm and dry for a night in the woods?

This is a challenging, sometimes uncomfortable and ultimately thrilling experience, spending the whole time outdoors and learning to fend for yourself. Are you up for the adventure?

Address Dryad Bushcraft, Swansea, +44 (0)1792 547213, www.dryadbushcraft.co.uk, info@dryadbushcraft.co.uk | Getting there Details on booking | Hours Visit website for information and to book a workshop | Tip The Roundhouse in Bishop's Wood is a great place to go to see green woodworking and have a campfire.

47_Gower Fresh Lavender
Purple Haze

The nature of farming has changed over the last few decades. Gone is the time when farmers could focus on growing crops or raising animals and expect to make a living from those activities alone. Over the years, farmers have started to diversify, perhaps operating a campsite from one of their fields or turning some of the farm buildings into holiday cottages. Some take their produce to farmers' markets so buyers know exactly where their food has come from.

And some have realised that if you have the right type of crop, you can encourage your customers to visit you. At Gower Fresh Lavender Fields, they have considered the visitor experience from start to finish. First, there is plenty of parking on site. Then, a tractor ride across the farm saves the walk to the lavender fields. Prepare to relax as the scent of the flowers wafts over you and the purple haze fills your vision. Some visitors sit in the rows of flowers, soaking up the sensation. Some lie down, looking up past the purple blooms to the sky. Young children run between the rows of flowers, laughing gleefully. Couples settle down for a romantic picnic with a stunning backdrop. This is the perfect place for some photos, with just the plants or one of the flower arches to frame the shot. Take your own or book in for a professional portrait of yourself, your family, or your dog.

Lavender is thought to improve a myriad of health conditions. The calming scent of lavender can help you to relax and sleep, creams with lavender oil are used to treat skin conditions, and the leaves make a fragrant tea. And standing in a field of lavender is guaranteed to lift your spirits!

After visiting the fields, you can stop for a tipple at the bar and maybe some live music before heading home from a lovely summer's day out, with a bunch of lavender and perhaps some fragrant gifts in hand.

Address Poundffald Farm, Three Crosses, Swansea, SA4 3PB, +44 (0)1792 712071, www.gowerfreshchristmastrees.co.uk, info@gowerfreshchristmastrees.co.uk | **Getting there** Bus 21 or 22 to Joiners Road; parking on site | **Hours** Dependent on flowering, usually June. Sun, Wed, Thu noon–8pm, Fri & Sat noon–6pm | **Tip** Poundffald Farm also has pick-your-own pumpkins and Christmas trees at the appropriate times of year, along with seasonal entertainment.

48　Gower Salt Marsh
Feasting on the fringe

The southern shore of the Gower Peninsula is characterised by cliffs and beaches pounded by waves. The northern coast is totally different. Sheltered from the waves by the sandbanks of Carmarthen Bay, silt has settled over thousands of years. This process has created mudflats and Atlantic salt meadows that form the largest ecosystem of this type in Wales.

At first glance, this landscape can appear bleak, but dig into the matter more closely, and its value becomes evident. The mud is home to large populations of molluscs such as cockles and mussels, crustaceans such as crabs and shrimp, and worms. The flat tops of the marshes are slashed with channels made by small creeks. The angled slopes and the way the air moves along these channels create a huge variety of microhabitats that are of national significance. The life within the mud supports birds such as oystercatchers and curlew. Large populations of overwintering birds, including geese and ducks, also tuck into the dwarf eelgrass, which lies flat on the sand when the tide is out, and rises up with the water.

The shrubby plants, many of which are covered by seawater at high tide, make for tasty grazing. Gower Salt Marsh Lamb has a Protected Designation of Origin (PDO), which means that the lambs must have been born, raised, slaughtered and butchered on the Gower Peninsula, and spent at least half their life (minimum of two months) grazing on the marshes. The lambs are fit because of the distance over which they forage, and their meat takes on some of the flavour of their varied salt meadow diet. For wildlife conservation, a fine balance is needed here. Some grazing increases the variety of plants, but over-grazing has the opposite, deleterious, effect. Now the lamb has been recognised for its unique flavour, local farmers have a good incentive to be responsible guardians of the land – it's a win for everyone.

Address The salt marshes occur all along the north coast of the Peninsula | Getting there Park in Crofty or along Marsh Road between Crofty and Llanrhidian (beware high tides – some areas flood) | Hours Accessible 24 hours | Tip The farm shop at Weobley Castle sells Gower Salt Marsh Lamb, and you can also buy it online (www.gowersaltmarshlamb.co.uk).

49 __ The Gravity Centre

Thrills and spills for everyone

In the 17th century, Isaac Newton, a so-so student at the University of Cambridge, was sent home when the college was closed due to an outbreak of bubonic plague. It was two years before he could return, but it seems that he flourished during this period of relative isolation. According to legend, this is when he watched an apple fall from a tree, wondered why it fell towards the Earth rather than at any other angle, and developed his Law of Universal Gravitation, which revolutionised our understanding of the forces governing our planet.

Is it mere coincidence, then, that the Gravity Centre at Weobley Castle is based on a field that used to be the castle's orchard? Or that fruit trees in the surrounding woods continue to drop apples downwards, in the same direction as the daredevils on wheels hare towards the Loughor Estuary?

You know you are about to do something exciting when you are fitted with a helmet and protection for your knees, elbows and wrists. Beginners start on a gentle slope with sledges. As you build your confidence, you can progress onto steeper areas and other equipment, such as mountain boards (like wheeled snowboards). As you develop your skills, you will become more graceful and able to tackle more challenging slopes. On a rainy day, the fun does not stop; the buggies are a popular option, as they slide and scoot over the slick grass.

Not sure about your ability? No worries; the instructors are experienced at working with all sorts of people, including those with physical and learning disabilities and neuro-diverse people.

Whatever the weather, you can feel the force and experience the fun of gravity, here in the old orchard. Given the choice, would Sir Isaac Newton have sat watching the apples fall or experienced the thrills of gravity for himself? I wonder whether Sir Isaac Newton would sit watching the apples fall or join those experiencing the thrills of gravity for themselves.

Address Weobley Castle, SA3 1HB, +44 (0)7856 152540, www.brdsports.co.uk, info@brdsports.co.uk | Getting there Bus 115 to Weobley Castle; free parking at the castle | Hours See website for details of coaching sessions | Tip If you fancy something a little more protected from the weather, the same crew organises 'Boardability' sessions for all abilities in Gorseinon. Contact details as above.

50 Hafod-Morfa Copperworks

A tarnished legacy

Although Swansea has no copper ore nearby, it was a centre for copper smelting from as early as 1717. A combination of abundant local coal reserves, a good port and copper mining over the Bristol Channel drove the growth of the industry that would give Swansea its moniker of 'Copperopolis'. By 1850, 11 significant copperworks resided along the River Tawe, processing over half the world's copper. Copper ore was imported by ship, turning Swansea into a major port. Coal was shipped down the Swansea Canal from mines in the Upper Swansea Valley to fuel the furnaces, which stood in rows inside the smelting halls and next to the rolling sheds.

At its industrial prime, this would have been a deeply unpleasant place. Multiple chimneys billowed smoke, polluting the air and making it hard to breathe. People were dwarfed by these massive buildings that were deafening and stifling to work in. Working conditions were not what we would expect today.

By the 1920s, copper smelting had ended, and the works switched to manufacturing copper products. By the 1960s, the area was largely derelict. In 1980, the last factory closed its doors and was abandoned. The industrial boom, while enriching a few, left this valley devoid of trees and heavily polluted. In partnership with local and national government, Swansea University brought together local volunteers, schoolchildren, members of the Territorial Army and others in the community under the banner of The Lower Swansea Valley Project to restore the area. Some buildings were demolished, others preserved. Pollutants were removed from the ground, trees were planted, and redevelopment created the Maritime Quarter, Parc Tawe, the sports stadium and a riverside trail. Although the project has come to an end, redevelopment work continues today.

Address Loverose Way, Swansea, SA1 2LE, www.hafodmorfacopperworks.com | Getting there Bus 34 or PR 2 to Landore Park & Ride; parking at Landore Park & Ride | Hours Accessible 24 hours | Tip Kilvey Hill offers a great vantage point from which to see the Lower Swansea Valley and beyond. Walk up from the car park near the junction of the A 4217 and B 5444 about one kilometre south of the distillery.

51 Hardings Down Hill Forts
Three for the price of one

It is not unusual to see a hill fort around the top of a hill in Britain. After all, there are more than 3,000 hill forts around the UK. What is unusual is to have three of them on one hilltop, none of which encircle the summit.

The Iron Age stretched from around 800 B.C. to A.D. 43. During this period, people were divided into rival tribal groups. Warfare was common as neighbouring tribes tried to steal cattle or slaves, or take control of resources, including territory. Forts were developed to protect a tribe from these aggressions. They would have been far more impressive then than they are now, after almost 2,000 years of abandonment. The ditches were deeper with steeper sides, and the central ring was fortified with a timber palisade. Visitors were corralled into the entrance area, which was more heavily fortified. Timber ornamentation probably adorned the gate area to evidence the wealth and skill of the tribe.

Some hill forts seem to have been lived in, and the north enclosure on Hardings Down has one visible house platform. Otherwise, they might have been used as a protection of last resort when an attack was imminent. One unusual feature of each of these three forts is that their entrances are not aligned to the east. Each has its entrance on the downhill side, which seems more practical than symbolic, as it's far harder to attack from below than above. Additional lines of bank and ditch can be seen on the east side of the western fort, distorting the familiar concentric rings. These are thought to be agricultural enclosures. The eastern fort is the largest but was never completed.

Hardings Down Hill forts are best viewed from the north, when the sun is low in the sky and shadows highlight the shape of the earthworks. There is also an older Bronze Age cairn on the hill, which appears to have been robbed at some point, and a standing stone of unknown age.

Address Near Hillside, Upper Hardingsdown, Llangennith, Gower, SA3 1JR | Getting there Bus 115 and 116 to Bellevue Farm, then a 15-minute walk; park near Hillside; north fort easily visible from the track to Hillside | Hours Accessible 24 hours | Tip The King's Head at Llangennith is a popular pub and hotel.

52 Helwick Lightship

A smashing rescue

This part of Britain's coastline is scattered with shipwrecks, partly due to shifting sandbanks that are not visible to approaching ships. Helwick Sands run for over six miles west from Port Eynon Point beyond the end of the Gower Peninsula. A lightship station was established here in 1846 to mark the position of the sandbank. Lightships did not have their own engines; they were towed into position by other vessels. So, when a huge storm hit the ship in 1908, it could not power itself out of trouble. The mast was smashed, as was the ship's lifeboat, and it started taking on water. A passing steamer saw its distress signal and sent a message to the lifeboat in Tenby. From there, it took the lifeboatmen two and a half hours to row out to the ship and rescue the seven men onboard.

The destroyed lightship was replaced by LV91. This was used to warn sailors to keep their distance until the late 1970s when it was replaced and towed to Swansea Marina, where it is now moored. Seven people worked and lived aboard, with 11 on the team in total. It must have been snug!

In the 1970s and 1980s, most lightships were decommissioned and replaced with light floats or Large Automatic Navigation Buoys (LANBYs). Those lightships that remain in use are no longer staffed, and most run from solar panels. This is, of course, a much cheaper option than a lightship with an 11-person crew.

The Helwick lightships were owned and operated by Trinity House, the UK's General Lighthouse Authority. It was incorporated by Henry VIII in 1514, and its work is paid for by 'light dues' paid by commercial ships visiting ports in the British Isles. The charity's full name is a mouthful: The Master, Wardens and Assistants of the Guild, Fraternity or Brotherhood of the most glorious and undivided Trinity and of St Clement in the Parish of Deptford Strond, in the County of Kent!

Address Tawe Basin, Maritime Quarter, Swansea, SA1 3XA | Getting there Bus 7 to Burrows Place, several to Sainsbury's Quay Parade; nearest parking at St David's multi storey | Hours Viewable from the outside only | Tip The lightship stands in front of the National Waterfront Museum.

53 Ivor Allchurch Statue
The golden boy of Welsh football

It was a different world back then. Footballers were permitted a maximum wage, which meant they had no financial incentive to switch clubs. This enabled Ivor Allchurch to spend much of his footballing career on home turf in Swansea. Despite losing the first two years of his professional footballing career to National Service, Ivor Allchurch remains the highest-scoring player of all time for the Swans, by a significant margin. During 1950–1951, Ivor was the youngest player ever to compete in every match through the season. He scored 186 goals for the club in 502 fixtures. His talent was not just restricted to Swansea: he also played for Wales, scoring 23 goals in 68 appearances. He represented Wales in the World Cup in 1958 when the team reached the quarter-finals. He was both a Swan and a Dragon of high repute. During his long career, he also had spells playing for Newcastle United and Cardiff.

It was a different world back then. Players in Swansea would walk to the matches alongside the fans. Ivor Allchurch used to walk with Esme, who became his wife in 1953. She remembers the fans asking him how he expected the match to go, as they headed towards the stadium together. Professional players always had matches on Christmas Day and Boxing Day. Of course, these would not be in the same place, so Christmas lunch was often hurried between one match and travelling to the other.

It was a different world back then. These days, professional footballers retire at the age of 35 on average. Ivor Allchurch loved playing football so much that he continued as a semi-professional until the age of 50. He was made a Member of the Most Excellent Order of the British Empire (MBE) for services to sport in 1966. Given that he was the golden boy of local football, it seems fitting to have his statue outside the Swans' stadium now. The only shame is that the statue is made from bronze, not gold!

Address Swansea.com Stadium, Landore, Swansea, SA1 2FA | Getting there Bus 4, 4A or X6 to Landore; nearest parking at Morfa Retail Park | Hours Accessible 24 hours, though access might be difficult on match days | Tip Rugby has also always been a popular sport in Swansea. St Helen's was the venue for Wales' first home international.

54 Joe's Ice Cream Parlour

A cool legacy

In the 1880s, life in much of Italy was hard. The country was in the middle of a population boom, poverty was rife, and Italians started to emigrate to find a better life. Now, around 80 million people across the world have Italian ancestors. This migration coincided with the Industrial Revolution in Wales, a booming local economy and the need for labour. The combination of circumstances inevitably led to an influx of Italian people.

One of these was Luigi Cascarini. He arrived in Swansea in 1898 and, coming from a country with a café culture, was shocked to find that there were no cafés to serve the needs of the newly bustling Swansea Valley. He opened a café in which he introduced the people of Swansea to the rich roast coffee flavours of Italy. He worked long hours, and the café became such a success that he opened another and another, and one café soon became a chain of cafés.

Once his eldest son Joe was old enough, Luigi collected him from Italy to help run the business. Joe's passion was not coffee but ice cream. He brought a secret recipe from home, sourced the very best ingredients he could find in Wales, and changed the café he ran into an ice cream parlour. The year was 1922 and the ice cream proved to be as popular as the coffee. For the next 40 years, Joe expanded the ice cream offering into the whole chain.

Joe died in 1968, but the ice cream parlours have continued to thrive and are still run by family members. Over the years, the business has diversified. It took a while to work out how to make soft scoop ice cream that tasted just as good as the original, but they succeeded in doing this in the 1970s, meaning they could sell the ice cream for people to take home. This led to Joe's Ice Cream being sold through supermarkets and even Harrods. The original recipe vanilla ice cream is still sold in Joe's Ice Cream parlours, alongside a variety of weird and wonderful new flavours.

Address 526 Mumbles Road, Swansea, SA3 4DH, www.joes-icecream.com | Getting there Bus 3, 3A or 113 to Oystermouth | Hours Daily 10.30am–5pm | Tip There are several Joe's Ice Cream Parlours around South Wales, including St Helen's Road, Swansea and Eastgate, Llanelli.

55 Kardomah Café
Doctor Who?

The Kardomah Café used to stand on Castle Street, not far from its current location. It was once part of a chain of iconic cafés but is now the only one left. In the 1930s, it was home to the Kardomah Gang – a group of local creatives, including poets, writers, composers and artists. Some of the names may be familiar: the poets Dylan Thomas and Vernon Watkins; the composer Daniel Jones; and the painter Mervyn Levy.

Like much of the rest of Swansea town centre, Castle Street was bombed in the Three Nights' Blitz on 19–21 February, 1941. Although the area had been targeted before, this was an extraordinary attack. A record 896 bombs landed on the town in those three nights, as the Luftwaffe tried to destroy the docks and train lines that supplied essential goods, such as coal. Tragically, 230 people were killed, over 400 were injured, and 7,000 were made homeless. Much of the town centre was razed to the ground, including the Kardomah Café.

With hindsight, this benefited the café – after the war, it was re-established using the latest 1950s' fashions, and the public area has been updated little since. The café remains an enclave of vintage 1950s' style – chequerboard formica tables with a coffee bean pattern, wooden panelling decorated with metallic reliefs and burgundy plastic-covered padded chairs. The cakes are even still presented to customers on a wooden trolley wheeled over to their tables.

The café has been used as a filming location for *Set Fire to the Stars*, a Welsh movie about Dylan Thomas, and in the *Dr Who* episode 'The End of Time: Part 1', where David Tennant and Bernard Cribbins have an emotionally-charged conversation over a drink. The café may be just as well known for the quality of its coffee and for being shortlisted by the *Daily Telegraph* as one of the best 50 coffee houses in the world.

Address 11 Portland Street, Swansea, SA1 3DH, +44 (0)1792 652336, www.kardomahcafé.com, kardomahcafé@yahoo.com | Getting there Bus to Kingsway Bus and Coach Station; train to Swansea, then a 10-minute walk | Hours Mon – Sat 8am – 3.30pm | Tip Another episode of *Dr Who* was filmed on the Swansea University Bay Campus.

56 Kenfig Castle
A foolish man builds his house on sand

After the Normans successfully invaded England, they set their sights on Wales. The Crown gifted land to Norman lords, but that land was not necessarily already part of the Norman kingdom. That was the case here in Kenfig, where the Norman Lord of Glamorgan built a castle to consolidate his power. This was seen as a place of strategic importance for the invasion, so he constructed the largest keep in the area. The stone tower was surrounded by eight acres of settlement protected by a timber palisade. Outside the palisade was a large sub-urb where crops were grown and livestock were reared to feed the townspeople.

Understandably, the Welsh locals did not take kindly to this inva-sion, and the town was subject to at least seven attacks, where parts – or all – of the settlement were razed to the ground. The keep survived every attack, and the town was repeatedly rebuilt. The castle was extended and altered over the course of three centuries, but eventually, both it and the town were abandoned and dismantled, the materials removed to be used elsewhere.

It was not the Welsh attacks that finally brought Kenfig to its knees, but sand. In the 14th century, areas of protective coastal flats were lost, making the coastline more vulnerable to erosion. Abnor-mally high tides then combined with periods of heavy rainfall and storms to de-stabilise previously dormant dunes. The sand became mobile and started to shift. It was not the sand ingress into buildings that first caused an issue, although it did create some work. Instead, it was the difficulty in growing crops when they were constantly being covered with sand. Land rents had to be dropped because the har-vests were poor, and ultimately, agriculture was abandoned. Without food, the settlement also had to be abandoned. Perhaps the Normans should have paid heed to the parable about a foolish man building his house on sand…

Address Ton Kenfig, Bridgend, CF33 4PR | Getting there Park near Prince of Wales Inn and walk for one kilometre approximately north across the nature reserve | Hours Accessible 24 hours | Tip A little further down the coast, it is possible to visit the dunes featured in *Lawrence of Arabia*, at Merthyr Mawr Nature Reserve, CF32 0ND.

57 Kenfig Dunes
Blooming sand-sational

If you were to look at Kenfig Dunes on a map, you might not choose to go there, as it is so close to the Port Talbot steelworks, a sprawling industrial complex emitting plumes of smoke and steam. It's not a promising start, but if you let that put you off, you will miss out.

Kenfig Dunes is a National Nature Reserve and Site of Special Scientific Interest for a reason. It forms part of Europe's most extensive dune system and provides habitats for a wide range of plants, animals and birds. The reserve is managed through grazing to allow the dunes to remain mobile, providing a mix of dune grassland, slacks (damp scrapes), scrub, salt marsh and beach.

In early summer, spires of purple orchid flowers pepper the dunes, but it is the altogether less-showy, pale yellow fen orchids found in the slacks that excite conservationists. Kenfig Dunes hosts the largest population of these rare orchids in the UK. Other species of conservation interest include the shrill carder bee, which is mainly straw-coloured with an orange tail, and the hairy dragonfly, which is black with blue spots and has an unmistakable hirsute thorax.

The largest natural lake in South Wales, Kenfig Pool, sits at one edge of the reserve. This is a magnet for birds, including bitterns, which make a distinctive booming sound in winter. Hides around the pool provide good bird-watching opportunities. With their long, downward-curving beaks, curlews are often seen on the beach, along with oystercatchers and other shoreline birds.

Numerous paths cross the dunes, and the Wales Coast Path runs along the seaward side. Walking can be hard going because the dunes are hilly and the sand soft, but the reward of spending time in this magical place is well worth the effort involved. And there's always a chance to recover with a coffee at the visitor centre or a beer pulled directly from the barrel in the Prince of Wales, accompanied by a pub lunch.

Address Kenfig Nature Reserve, Ton Kenfig, CF33 4PT, +44 (0)1656 530089,
www.kenfigcorporationtrust.co.uk | Getting there Park at Kenfig NNR car park,
CF33 4PT | Hours Accessible 24 hours | Tip The dunes have a long shoreline over-
looking Swansea Bay – perfect for a picnic on the beach.

58 Kenfig Town Hall
A not-so-new house

After Kenfig was inundated with sand, it was incorporated with the nearby town of Maudlam. Early in the 17th century, funds were raised for a new town hall, and the borough of Kenfig became independent again.

The pub next to the new town hall was known as 'Ty Newydd', which means 'New House'. Both the inn and the town hall were extensively rebuilt two centuries later. Perhaps the owner thought that a 200-year-old establishment should no longer be referred to as 'new', as it was renamed 'The Prince of Wales' in 1822 in honour of the recently-crowned George IV. The town hall was probably built on pillars to enable a market or other town activities underneath. It might only be used for functions today, but it has had a colourful history. It was where the portreeve (the official with authority over the town) conducted the borough's business, including trade and enforcing expected behavioural standards for individuals and businesses. Monthly Manorial Courts were held here from 1672, and a Sunday school operated from the hall for over 130 years. The portreeve was also the town's coroner, so inquests were held here. When shipwrecks washed mariners onto the nearby shore, the hall was used as a mortuary until the bodies could be buried. It's no surprise that the building is reputedly haunted!

On a happier note, the hall was home to an annual festival, Gŵyl Mabsant, in honour of the local patron saint. Candlelight suffused the room with a warm glow, a harpist provided music and locals danced the night away, no doubt enlivened by beverages from the adjoining inn.

These days, the room is still used for special events that are supplied with food and drink from the Prince of Wales Inn. The pub prides itself on its family-friendliness and is one of the few places left where your pint is poured straight from the barrel.

Address Prince of Wales Inn, Kenfig, Bridgend, CF3 4PR, +44 (0)1656 740356,
www.princeofwalesinn.co.uk | Getting there Bus 63 to Heol Llan Junction, then a
1.75 kilometre walk; parking on site | Hours Bar Mon 4–10pm, Tue–Sun noon–11pm;
food Tue–Sat noon–2.30pm & 5–8pm, Sun 12.30pm onwards | Tip The propeller in the
garden broke off the SS *Tillamook* when she ran aground in 1946.

59 — Labyrinth
A community pilgrimage

The terms 'labyrinth' and 'maze' are often used interchangeably, although labyrinths generally only have one route, and mazes have many. Mazes are designed to confound, to ensure that anyone who enters becomes lost. Confounding factors in mazes can include dead ends and looping sections that frustratingly bring you back to somewhere you have already been. The first mazes were not designed to be cracked; they were set up to protect the tombs of wealthy Egyptians from being raided. Raiders would first have to find their way into the tomb, then find their way out again with the booty. A long ball of string would have come in handy! Mazes that confound developed into a form of entertainment when they started to be used in formal gardens, with hedges as walls to hide the way.

In contrast, when you step into a labyrinth, you can usually see the whole of your route, but that does not matter. If you continue to follow the path, you will eventually reach your goal. It is thought that when the Crusades made a pilgrimage to the holy land too dangerous, the church adopted the pagan use of labyrinths. Walking the convoluted route of a labyrinth enabled the devout to take a spiritual journey without risking their lives. Labyrinths can often be found in churches, including the cathedral at St David's. Turf labyrinths with a path mown through longer grass have been used in Europe since at least the 15th century. Adding to the nomenclature confusion, these are often known as 'mizmazes'.

The only labyrinth in Swansea is in Rosehill Quarry Community Garden. Every year, community members trim the grass and relay the cockleshell path that circles and turns back on itself multiple times before eventually reaching the middle. This brings the community together and encourages visitors to take their time in the park, be mindful of the insects buzzing in the trees, and embark on their own mini-pilgrimage.

Address Terrace Road, Swansea, SA1 6HU, www.rosehillquarry.org | Getting there Bus 49 to Rose Hill Top; some on-street parking nearby | Hours Unrestricted | Tip A stone spiral that feels similar to the labyrinth sits at one end of the stepping stones across Pennard Pill at Three Cliffs Bay.

60 Llanelli North Dock

From mud flats to Blue Tits

Coal was once brought from the nearby collieries down to the mud flats of the Lliedi estuary, where boats would beach for loading. The tidal range here is significant; it must have been some feat to get the timing of landing, loading and setting off again just right. Eventually, a series of docks were built. Still, by the end of the 19th century, these were not big enough for the volume of coal that was being exported.

Early in the 20th century, plans were drawn up to build North Dock. Understandably, the people still operating shipping from the stages just downstream were unhappy about the disruption to their business. After some legal wrangling and associated delays, the dock was finally opened a couple of days before Christmas in 1903, when the SS *Gazelle* was the first ship through the gates.

The dock was mainly used to export coal, but it did occasionally have some side gigs. For example, in 1922, it became home to HMS *Chester*, the biggest ship ever to sail into the port. The *Chester* had done its service in the Battle of Jutland and was moved to Llanelli for scrapping. During World War II, the area around the dock was used to store goods. Consequently, it was bombed in 1940, causing a massive fire. The US Army also trained here during their preparations for D-Day. A couple of years after the dock closed for coal exports in 1951, 19 landing craft were stored here, this time to be moth-balled and maintained rather than scrapped. And it was done well; when the ships were called back into service in the 1956 Suez Crisis, all 19 sailed out, ready for use once again.

These days, the dock is busy with a somewhat different range of activities. The artificial beach and (relatively) safe waters are attractive to swimmers (the Blue Tits are often seen swimming here, even on the coldest of mornings), paddleboarders, kayakers and even an occasional Zorber.

Address Traeth Fford, Llanelli, SA15 2LY | Getting there Train to Llanelli (2 kilometres away); park at Millennium Quay car park, SA15 2LF | Hours Accessible 24 hours | Tip There are no lifeguards at North Dock. Visit the RNLI website for details of local beaches with lifeguards (www.rnli.org).

61 Llanelly House
Wales' Finest Georgian Building

Was it a ghost who started the fire in Llanelly House's plant room in 2023? The insurance assessors did not think so, but then 'misbehaving ghosts' are not usually included in the possible list of causes of insurance claims. Luckily, although there was damage to the costumes worn by staff, the fabric of the building was largely unharmed, and this gem remains standing – complete with its ghost…

During the coronavirus pandemic, when the building was locked and unused, the trustees had to visit every weekday to satisfy the insurers that the building was secure. One Friday, the trustee responsible walked around the building, noting that everything was in order. When he returned the following Monday to check again, the attic room was not as he had left it. This room was set up to show how it had been when the house's resident ghost was alive. Over the weekend, the bed had been moved to the opposite side of the room, and other exhibits had been rearranged. Was the ghost suggesting that she had the furniture organised differently? This trustee was the last person to have been in that room; the building had been locked for the entire weekend, and the keycard system had not recorded any other visitors. What other explanation could there have been?

Whether or not you believe in ghosts, Llanelly House is an interesting place to visit for a guided tour. You can learn about the wealthy Stepney family and the different roles the building has played in the town, from knowledgeable costumed guides. The house was built in 1714 by the local Member of Parliament, and if the walls could talk, they would have plenty of tales to tell of the 300-plus years since then.

Llanelly House is now owned by a charitable trust that supports its work by operating as a venue for special events and housing a bistro where you can relax with a coffee or be entertained at one of their themed evenings.

Address Bridge Street, Llanelli, SA15 3UF, +44 (0)1554 772857, www.llanelly-house.org.uk, bookings@llanellyhouse.org.uk | Getting there Bus L4 or L6 to British Legion or Court House; several town centre parking options; train to Llanelli, then a 1.3 kilometre walk | Hours Mon–Sat 9.30am–4pm (see website for seasonal hours) | Tip If you like to visit haunted buildings, the ghost of a gamekeeper who was murdered by a poacher is reported to have been seen on the staircase at Margam Castle near Port Talbot.

62   Lliw Reservoirs
Accessible adventure

The Lliw reservoirs have been supplying drinking water to Swansea's residents for over 150 years. Just a short drive from the city centre, they now provide a fantastic recreational resource as well as drinking water.

Although swimming is not permitted, you can hire or self-launch stand-up paddleboards or kayaks in the lower reservoir. If you prefer a more restful activity, fishing is also allowed. The lower reservoir has a footpath running all the way around it, which is about three kilometres long. This path is narrow in places and can be uneven underfoot. The eastern side of the reservoir sports a series of oak sculptures depicting native wildlife. These have been carved using a chainsaw and other tools by the Swansea sculptor Ami Marsden. They include a rabbit, heron, trout, hedgehog, otter, red kite and pipistrelle bats. The tree-lined banks provide beautiful reflections on a still day.

The upper reservoir can be reached using the Two Reservoirs Trail. This is a there-and-back route that is well surfaced and has a gentle incline. This makes it accessible for people using wheelchairs, prams or bikes. The total distance is five kilometres. The local bird life includes birds of prey such as peregrines, kestrels and red kites, and others such as whinchats – which are endangered – and curlew.

Activity sheets and a playground provide entertainment for younger children, and the café offers somewhere to warm up after a crisp winter's walk or paddle.

This recreational development is among several around Welsh Water reservoirs supporting the Wellbeing of Future Generations (Wales) Act 2015. This is world-leading legislation that puts Wales at the forefront of sustainable development. One of the requirements is for public bodies to consider the long-term impacts of their decisions on future generations, and opening up places like this will undoubtedly have a positive impact.

Address Felindre, Swansea, SA5 7NP, www.lliwreservoirs.com | Getting there On-site parking | Hours Daily 8am–6pm | Tip For more forest trails and mountain bike routes, head to Afan Forest Park near Port Talbot.

63 Loughor Castle
A bargain unleashed

The Romans were the first people we know of who built a fortification on this site. A little further east, the Ordnance Survey maps mark the site of 'Roman practice works'. This is where soldiers practised building forts to support their invasion of what was to become known as Britannia. The corners were the hardest thing to get right, so that is what they practised, creating several small square structures, the footprints of which remain just visible from the air. At Loughor, a complete fort, known as 'Leucarum', was built, probably to control the low-tide ford of the estuary here.

A millennium or so later, long after the Romans had left and their stone fort had collapsed, the Normans arrived and built a wooden fortification on the same site. They probably had similar reasons, in addition to asserting their authority, as they extended their invasion from England to Wales. The Welsh were not too happy about this incursion into their country and burnt the castle down around 1150. Nevertheless, the area remained under Norman control. The castle was rebuilt in stone in the 12th and 13th centuries by the de Braose family, who were given the Gower Peninsula by King John. The de Braoses were not known for their loyalty, and promptly upset the king by siding with the powerful Welsh prince Llywelyn ap Iorwerth.

The castle became less important after Edward I finally beat the Welsh in 1283. The de Braoses still owned it and, in 1302, started to rent it out. The rent might be seen as symbolic: one greyhound collar a year. In medieval times, only the nobility were allowed to own greyhounds, so although a collar might not have been of significant value, it would undoubtedly have reminded tenants of their place in society. With the rental income so low, it is no surprise that the castle was not maintained – and today, it is just part of one tower and some foundations that remain.

Address Castle Street, Loughor, Swansea, SA4 6TS, www.cadw.gov.wales | Getting there Bus 111 or X11 to Ship & Castle; on-street parking | Hours Accessible 24 hours | Tip There is only one greyhound stadium left in Wales, at Ystrad Mynach, north of Caerphilly.

64 Machynys Monk's Island
Greener greens

Standing on the first-floor balcony overlooking Machynys golf course and the Loughor Estuary, it is hard to imagine what this landscape looked like just a few decades ago. For around a century, Machynys was an industrial hot spot. Four brickworks once operated here, using clay dug from pits that now form the golf course's ponds. Alongside the brickworks stood a tinplate works, replete with railway lines and a dock, and workers were housed in brick terraces in two distinct communities: Machynys and Bwlch Y Gwynt. It was noisy, smelly and dirty, and the air was often thick with smoke. Ships arrived with raw materials and left with coal and processed metal.

Now, the housing has been replaced with New England-style homes, and the industry has been replaced with one of the greenest golf courses in the country. Around half the course is designated as a habitat for wildlife and one of the clay pit lakes is a Site of Special Scientific Interest, protected because it provides a home to 13 different species of dragonfly. In 2023, the club became GEO certified, a standard that requires good environmental management and social responsibility practices. The Championship golf course was designed by Jack Nicklaus and provides plenty of challenges, particularly with the number of water features golfers need to negotiate. There is also a state-of-the-art driving range where visitors can play a virtual round on some of the major golf courses across the world.

The club is open to non-members, and if you don't play golf, you can still visit the restaurant, spa and gym. The spa offers a range of treatments such as massages, salt scrubs and facials, and facilities such as a spa pool, sauna, aromatherapy room and steam room. The first-floor bar/restaurant is popular for both its food and the glorious views across this transformed landscape and the Loughor Estuary.

Address Nicklaus Avenue, Llanelli, SA15 2DG, www.machynys.com | Getting there Train to Llanelli (two kilometres away); parking on site | Hours Brasserie Mon 8am–5pm, Tue & Wed 8am–6pm, Thu–Sat 8am–8pm; bar 7am–late; spa by appointment | Tip If adventure golf is more your thing, check out Bunkers in Swansea City Centre.

65 Mad Mouse Roller Coaster
A wild ride

Since we significantly reduced the threat of predators, life has become much safer for humans. Many people miss the thrill of fear and seek scary activities for a buzz. Some follow dangerous pursuits like riding fast motorbikes or climbing without ropes. Others choose safer pursuits that just give the impression of danger, like riding on roller coasters.

The precursors of roller coasters were first built in the 17th century in palace gardens around St Petersburg. These featured a steep arcing slope covered in ice during the winter. Aristocrats would climb to the top and slide down the ice. Catherine the Great enjoyed this so much that she wanted a summer version, too. This led to the development of roller coasters with wheels. In 1784, the first two were opened in her gardens. One featured a long, steep slope followed by a series of humps; the other was a spiral. A century later, roller coasters were available in several places in Europe.

Meanwhile, thrill seekers in the United States had discovered the gravity railroads built to transport ore from mines. The Americans soon took the lead in roller coaster design. In 1885, the first complete circuit was opened on Coney Island. In 1959, Disneyland started using tubular steel tracks, which opened up the possibility of more convoluted rides.

The highest roller coaster in the world is at Six Flags in New Jersey. Kingda Ka boosts riders from stationary to over 200 kilometres (128 miles) per hour in only 3.5 seconds. From the high point of 139 metres (456 feet), the equivalent of 45 storeys, passengers plunge vertically back to ground level.

Riding the Mad Mouse roller coaster at the Gateway Resort, you will not break any height or speed records. However, even a relatively small roller coaster like this gives riders a thrill; for many, that is just what they are looking for.

Address Gateway Resort, Millennium Coastal Path, Bynea, SA14 9SN, +44 (0)1554 771202, www.gatewayresort.co.uk, info@gatewayresort.co.uk | Getting there No public transport nearby; plentiful parking on site | Hours See website for seasonal hours | Tip If you and your family like a thrill, have you tried climbing? Flashpoint Swansea is in Parc Tawe in the centre of Swansea and has facilities for all ages (www.crazyclimbswansea.com).

66 Meridian Tower

It's lonely at the top

The Meridian Tower stands proudly between Swansea Marina and the waterfront, dwarfing all other buildings in the city and commanding the skyline. Its windows and white cladding gleam in the sun, drawing the eye. It seems incredibly tall, standing at 107 metres (29 storeys). It towers above the rest of the marina and the rest of the city but is not just the tallest building in Swansea: it is the tallest building in Wales by a considerable margin – the tallest in Cardiff is more than 20 metres shorter, standing at 85 metres.

The definition of a skyscraper continues to grow. If you count any building higher than 100 metres, which some do, then it is the only skyscraper in the whole of Wales. It looks impressive, and it is impressive.

That is until you compare it to some of the other skyscrapers in the world. The Shard in London stands at 309 metres – almost three times the height of the Meridian Tower. The Burj Khalifa in Dubai is over twice the height of The Shard, rising to a dizzying 828 metres. Even St Paul's Cathedral in London, built in 1710, is some four metres taller than the Meridian Tower. That really was a feat of engineering.

Nevertheless, the Meridian Tower is an impressive feature of the Swansea skyline and is elegant in its own way. Maybe it was the thin air at such a height that got to the heads of the armed men who held diners hostage in the top-floor restaurant in 2014. Luckily, after hours of negotiations, the siege ended with no casualties. At the time of writing, the restaurant is closed, but when it reopens, diners will no doubt be delighted with the views over the entire bay and the city. The residents of its 123 apartments surely are. After all, it is not the actual height of a building that makes it seem impressive; it is its height compared to its neighbours, and views that are unrestricted by other buildings.

Address Trawler Road, Maritime Quarter, Swansea, SA1 1JN | **Getting there** Bus 7 to Marriott Hotel; park at Paxton Street car park, SA1 | **Hours** Viewable from the outside only | **Tip** Although the restaurant at the top of the tower is no longer open, there are several in the area, including El Pescador at the base of the tower.

67 Millennium Coastal Path
Birds, beaches and sunsets

The Wales Coast Path was the first long-distance trail in the world to run around an entire country's coastline. The Millennium Coastal Path provides 13 smooth, tarmacked miles of the 870-mile trail, as it runs from Loughor past Llanelli to Pembrey. The section of the path running past Llanelli is particularly attractive for both walkers and cyclists. From the south, it follows the line of the scalloped beaches at Machynys, past some impressive beach-front homes. At the end of the houses, it turns along the Lliedi tidal mud flats. When the tide is in, these shimmer with reflected light. When the tide is out, they provide a restaurant to hundreds of seabirds that feast on the diverse life that inhabits the mud. In fact, the wetlands that these mudflats are a part of are designated as a Ramsar site – of international importance because of the number of birds that live or visit here.

The route then passes North Dock and St Elli's Bay, where you can pick up a cup of tea or an ice cream. The next section of the Millennium Coastal Path weaves along the seafront, where locals congregate on a fine day to watch the sun set over Carmarthen Bay. The beach here is dangerous to swim from – most locals swim in North Dock instead. However, the large expanse of flat sand does provide an excellent place for children (or adults) to play.

Shortly after rising over the railway line, the path continues around the bay. There is also an option to detour inland past the Eisteddfod stones to Sandy Water Park, where the path circles the lake. Here, ducks, geese and swans flock to the water and often raise broods of young.

Platforms along the Millennium Coastal Path provide seating with fine views across the bay, overlooking the Gower Peninsula to the south and Pembrey to the north. On a very clear day, Tenby is also visible in the far distance.

Address Llanelli seafront, SA15 | **Getting there** Train to Llanelli (two kilometres away); park at Millennium Quay car park, SA15 2LF | **Hours** Accessible 24 hours | **Tip** The Sandpiper Brewers Fayre pub has a garden overlooking the lake in Sandy Water Park.

68 Mission Gallery

Prayer, punk and paintings

The contrast between the dour stone exterior and the light and airy interior of this building could not be greater. St Nicholas Church was built in 1868 as a non-denominational seaman's mission, providing services and religious succour to those far from home. The mission activities were transferred to a building near the New Cut Bridge in 1919. During World War II, the mission was bombed once in that building and again in the next building it occupied. It moved to 'The Flying Angel' on Prince of Wales Dock as a temporary measure – actually staying for 50 years before moving to King's Dock and eventually closing in 2010.

Meanwhile, St Nicholas Church survived the Blitz. It was used as a warehouse, a photography studio and even an underground punk venue called 'The Crypt' before the council offered it to some local artists in the 1970s. Those artists rolled up their sleeves (literally) and renovated the building into a beautiful gallery space. Glenys Cour was among their number. She was still painting in 2024, when the gallery held an exhibition – full of vibrant and exciting work – in honour of her hundredth birthday.

The main gallery space is not always full of light; the artists are welcome to reimagine it as they see fit, as long as they comply with the building's Grade II-listed status. In the past, it has been painted black. On another occasion, it revelled in rainbow stripes. Sometimes, paintings line the walls. At other times, artworks hang from the ceiling or stand to fill the 'cathedral' space.

The main gallery is complemented by the 'Maker' alcove and 'The Wall', which allow for smaller exhibitions. Most exhibitions are of works by emerging and established artists who are either Welsh or live locally.

The gallery also hosts workshops, performances focusing on Welsh language and culture, and films created by artists.

Address Gloucester Place, Swansea, SA1 1TY, +44 (0)1792 652016, www.missiongallery.co.uk, info@missiongallery.co.uk | **Getting there** Bus 7 to Burrows Place; several car parks nearby | **Hours** Wed–Sat 11am–5pm | **Tip** Tides Gallery in Mumbles has a wide range of art for sale from over 30 emerging fine artists (624 Mumbles Road).

69 Môr Hapus

Happy Sea, Happy Me

Every time we visit a beach, we have an impact. The Môr Hapus Project helps us to unearth the world beneath the waves and understand how we can make that impact positive. The team found a Tip Top ice lolly wrapper on one of their two-minute beach cleans in 2021. Nothing unusual there, you might think, as snack-related litter is not uncommon on popular beaches. Except, the price was clearly printed on the plastic wrapper. It was 2d. That's tuppence in old money. Very old money. The UK decimalised its currency in 1971, making this wrapper, which was still in tip-top condition, at least 50 years old. Maybe we should think twice before discarding our plastic waste.

Other plastics are also a challenge to marine life, including ghost nets and fishing lines. They are strong and long lasting and can wrap themselves around the necks or bodies of sea creatures, causing them to suffer in unimaginable ways.

But it is not all about the bad stuff; Môr Hapus also helps people develop a sense of wonder about the ocean. Have you ever wished that the critters in rock pools would not hide as soon as you peer in? The team at Môr Hapus will spend time with you, showing you what is what in the rockpool itself. They will then carefully catch some of the critters that usually hide or move so fast you can't see them properly, and put them in an aquarium for close inspection. At first, the water is murky with salt and sand, but it does not take long for the murk to start to clear and the different fish and shellfish to become more visible. Watch spellbound as they move around the aquarium, and the Môr Hapus team identifies the different species for you.

Môr Hapus also works on climate and pollution impact projects, like collecting microplastics from sand. The organisation is always keen to hear from groups who would like a more in-depth exploration of the beach at Bracelet Bay or further afield.

Address Bracelet Bay, by appointment only, +44 (0)7856 152540, www.morhapus.org |
Getting there Bus 3 or 3A to Pier Hotel; park at Bracelet Bay car park, SA3 4JT or nearby
on road | Hours By appointment only | Tip If you like eating seafood, check out the Seafood
Hut on Promenade Terrace, Mumbles (summer only).

70 Mumbles Lighthouse

A solar-powered sentinel

The Bristol Channel has a tidal range of between 12 and 14 metres – the second highest in the world. Combined with strong currents, rocky reefs and sandbanks, it makes this stretch of water notoriously difficult to navigate. For centuries, lighthouses have helped mariners by signalling particular hazards. In 1791, when it was decided to build a lighthouse on a rocky island off Mumbles, there were already two nearby. One had a single lamp, and the other had two separate towers. To distinguish it from the others, Mumbles Lighthouse was built with two lights, one above the other.

However, it was not the lights that provided the lighthouse with its first distinguishing moment. That happened when it collapsed before it was even opened. Luckily, the second construction was more robust and has been in operation for over 230 years. Initially, the two lights were created by burning coal. It did not take long for the operators to realise that that created an awful lot of work and expense. The lights were replaced by a single oil-powered lamp, which a light-house keeper fired up every evening. In the 1990s, the lamp was upgraded again, this time to run on solar power, and it is now oper-ated remotely – by someone in Essex.

The dark stone construction around the base of the lighthouse is the remains of a Palmerston Fort. It is one of many built after the 1860 Royal Commission on the Defence of the United Kingdom recommended their construction to protect against a feared French invasion. Over time, the threat of invasion disappeared, but sadly, the rather brutalist constructions have remained.

It is possible to reach the lighthouse island at low tide, where you can see the remains of the lighthouse keeper's house as well as the base of the lighthouse and fort. You can also quickly become cut off as the sea rises rapidly here, so please be careful if you decide to take a closer look.

Address Mumbles, Swansea, SA3 4EN | Getting there Bus 3 or 3A to Pier Hotel; park at Bracelet Bay car park, SA3 4JT or nearby on road | Hours Viewable from the outside only | Tip The Lighthouse restaurant on the far side of Bracelet Bay has good food and fantastic views of the lighthouse and the Bristol Channel.

71_Mumbles Pier
The heroines of 1883

Imagine living in the small village of Mumbles in 1883. Fashionable women are taking up more than their fair share of pavements with long, full skirts. Corsets are *de rigueur*. Women are meant to be pretty, demure and quiet. It is a man's world, and a girl's success relies on finding a good husband. But no fashionable women are taking a stroll along the front today; everyone who can is hunkering down behind closed doors, with fires lit in the hearth.

A storm has been raging for two days, throwing waves and rain at the village. Ships' captains have been caught out and are desperately battling the conditions all around the UK. Your father is the lighthouse keeper, making sure the warning lights keep burning. But in conditions like this, knowing there are hazards and successfully avoiding them are two entirely different matters.

A German barque has hit the rocks below the lighthouse, and the lifeboat has been launched. You wish you could be sitting patiently by the fire, waiting for the storm to pass, but you must do something. The lifeboat is now wrecked, too, and men are floundering in the water. You run down to the pier with your sister, clothes plastered to your body by the wind and rain, ignoring your father's pleas to stay safe. You tie your shawls together and risk your own lives to save two of the crew members by hauling them out of the water and onto the pier.

Remarkably, by today's standards at least, the two women received no recognition at all from the Royal National Lifeboat Institution despite having saved two of the lifeboat crew. Instead, the Ace sisters had to rely on the Empress of Germany to show her gratitude for helping her subjects. Now, there is a blue plaque near the pier, recognising the courage of these two women, who could have chosen to stay at home and look pretty, but instead risked their lives to save others.

Address Mumbles Road, Mumbles, Swansea, SA3 4EN, www.mumbles-pier.co.uk | Getting there Bus 3 or 3A to Pier Hotel; parking available on Mumbles Road | Hours Amusements Sun–Thu 10am–8pm, Fri & Sat 10am–10pm; café Sun–Thu 9am–6pm, Fri & Sat 9am–7pm | Tip The lifeboat station at the end of the pier is usually open to visitors from 11am–5pm.

72 Neath Abbey
The great land-grab

After the Norman Invasion of England in 1066 and their subsequent incursion into Wales, the land was divided up between powerful Norman lords. The Pope had supported the invasion in exchange for an agreement that William the Conqueror would reform the church in Britain, bringing it in line with the rest of the Catholic Church. Hence, the Normans built a flurry of monasteries as they worked their way across the country, and Neath Abbey is one of these.

Norman knight Sir Richard de Grenville was given the land upon which the abbey now stands and founded the monastery in 1130. It started life as a centre for monks from the Savigniac Order, but this was soon subsumed into the Cistercian Order. The monastery was granted lands in Devon and Somerset as well as Glamorgan, which together provided a massive opportunity for it to prosper from farming and mining activities. And prosper it did. By the late 13th century, Neath Abbey was one of the wealthiest in Wales. Around 50 monks were based at the abbey, supported by lay brothers to manage the estates. This wealth is reflected in the size, number and quality of the buildings we can see on the site today.

The Catholic monasteries were dissolved when Henry VIII fell out with the Pope and created the Church of England in the 16th century. Many of the buildings were demolished so they could not be used again, which is why there are so many ruinous abbeys in Britain. On this site, many of the walls remained, and the new owners built a mansion in the old cloisters, which they used for a century or so before it was abandoned.

The next significant impact on the site was from the Industrial Revolution when copper smelting works were built on abbey land. Luckily, parts of the original buildings survived. The impressive remains are now looked after by the Welsh government through Cadw.

Address Monastery Road, Neath, SA10 7DR, www.cadw.gov.wales | Getting there Several buses go to Smiths' Arms; some parking on site | Hours Daily 10am–4pm | Tip The disbanding of the monasteries did not mark the end of Catholicism in Britain. The Menevia Cathedral Church of St Joseph's in Swansea is now the centre of Catholicism in the area.

73 Neath Abbey Ironworks
Dragon's breath forging history

The former ironworks at Neath Abbey are impressive even today. Imagine what it was like here when the two enormous blast furnaces were fired up, and materials were being shifted around; busy, noisy and smelly, the sky dark with smoke.

It is even more impressive when you realise how important this small site was in powering the first Industrial Revolution – and Wales' place as the world's first industrialised nation. Around 8,000 engineering plans from these ironworks have been preserved for products as diverse as steam engines and ships.

Clydach Mill already stood on this site when the land was granted to Richard de Granville after the Norman Conquest. He, in turn, granted it to Neath Abbey. From the late 18th century, copper ore from Cornwall was being traded with Welsh coal, and Neath was an attractive site to make the most of the industry. It was close to the port of Swansea to import raw materials, the river provided water power, the nearby forests provided a source of charcoal, and local mines provided coal. By 1800, only 2,000 steam engines existed; most power was derived directly from wind or watermills, which limited the places it could be used. Neath Abbey Ironworks became a world leader in manufacturing beam engines (a form of steam engine) that were highly efficient and enabled industrial processes to be developed all around the world, including Europe, Asia, Australasia and South America. These could be used in places where water or wind were not abundant.

The ironworks also produced the parts needed for town gas works, where coal was burnt to create a gas used for fuel and lighting in municipalities. Luckily, natural gas replaced this toxic gas when reserves were found in the North Sea. We are now up to the fourth industrial revolution, and this site sits in graceful retirement again, devoid of the thuds, clanks and blasts of heavy industry.

Address New Road, Neath Abbey, Neath, SA10 7NH | **Getting there** Several buses go to Smiths' Arms; some on-street parking nearby. Head north on the drive between industrial units for about 50 metres | **Hours** Viewable from the outside only | **Tip** There is a popular fish and chip shop almost opposite the entrance to the ironworks – Abbey Fish Bar.

74 Neath Abbey Waterfall

A powerful force in a peaceful valley

Walking through the ruinous buildings of Neath Abbey Ironworks to reach the River Clydach and its waterfalls gives you a strong hint of the valley's industrial past. This feeling quickly erodes as you walk up the river running through a steep-sided valley to the waterfall. It feels like it is a million miles from any city or industry, decked in trees and full of the sounds of water and birdsong. The valley has been formed by water running over the rocks for millennia, since well before humans started the Industrial Revolution. From below, the waterfall appears to be natural, with the river cascading over dark chunks of rock and then continuing its journey to the sea. It is not until you reach the top of the fall and look down that you can clearly see the elegant curved weir forming the lip of the upper pool.

From medieval times, a watermill operated in this valley, and in 1825, the forge and rolling mill at Neath Abbey Ironworks were powered by water. This meant they needed water from higher up the valley to create a drop powerful enough to turn the wheel. Handily, there was already a waterfall here; they only needed to add a dam across the top of the falls and feed water along a leat to the wheel. This is why the waterfall looks so natural for most of its height.

Ironically, although a watermill was needed to power the ironworks at first, the ironworks made steam engines that, in turn, made watermills largely obsolete by enabling power production anywhere it was required. Watermills were often put to more than one use through their lifetime, and this one was no exception. The building spent the first 50 years or so of its life powering the ironworks and the next century operating as a woollen mill. It was not until 1974 that the building was retired from use, and the valley became a peaceful haven once again, devoid of the thuds, clanks and blasts of heavy industry.

Address New Road, Neath Abbey, Neath, SA10 7NH | Getting there Several buses go to Smiths' Arms; some on-street parking nearby. Head north on the drive between industrial units for about 50 metres to Neath Abbey Ironworks, then continue under the viaduct for another 250 metres to the waterfall | Hours Accessible 24 hours | Tip Keep following the path up the river to visit more waterfalls.

75 North Dock Engine House
A head for heights?

As you look across the water of North Dock from the beach, it is easy for the eye to be fooled into thinking there is a church tower on the skyline. With a closer look, it appears to be a little more stark than a church tower, a little more industrial. And indeed, it is.

When the dock was in use, it was kept full of water to keep the ships afloat. This required a dock gate that was sturdy enough to hold back a vast volume of water and the weight of loaded cargo ships. This made the gate exceptionally heavy, which meant that it could not be operated by hand.

The tower was built to house a hydraulic accumulator – an early energy storage system. Water from a reservoir was pumped into a cylinder in the tower, with a non-return valve that stopped the water from flowing back into the reservoir. This meant that when the cylinder was topped with weights, it put the water under immense pressure. When a lever was pulled (or pushed), the water pressure was enough to either open or close the heavy dock gates. Of course, this manoeuvre was only done when the tide was high, or the water would have flowed out of the dock like a tidal wave. The same system was used to power other plant around the dock, such as the cranes.

The hydraulic accumulator process is not dissimilar to that used to store wind and solar energy now. When there is excess energy in the grid, water is pumped up to reservoirs such as Ben Cruachan in Scotland. When a spike in demand cannot be met by supply, the water is released. There is enough power in the released water to turn electricity-generating turbines (rather than opening or closing lock gates), and that electricity can be put into the grid. In this example, the water is raised to such a height that no additional weight needs to be applied.

In 2009, the building was refurbished and now houses a popular American-themed restaurant.

Address Pump House, North Dock, Llanelli, SA15 2LF; restaurant: +44 (0)1554 897771, www.facebook.com/cattleandcollanelli | **Getting there** Train to Llanelli (two kilometres away); park at Millennium Quay car park, SA15 2LF | **Hours** Viewable from the outside only; restaurant daily noon–11pm | **Tip** Cattle & Co also has a restaurant on York Street, Swansea.

76 Oystermouth Castle
A ghost of angels

The history of Oystermouth Castle is not dissimilar to that of many Norman fortresses in Wales. It was first built in the decades following the Norman Conquest of England when the Normans were trying to assert their rule over the Welsh. This proved a little more difficult than the conquest of England, and many of their castles saw several attacks by the Welsh before the nation finally capitulated.

The first castle was constructed by William de Londres of Ogmore (a Norman) in the early 12th century. It probably had a stone keep and a rubble stone rampart and gate tower, but all that stone didn't prove to be much use against the Welsh; it was first lost to them in 1116. As time progressed, the fortifications were strengthened, attacked, lost and regained several times.

During the medieval period, the aristocracy held an immense amount of power. The de Braoses held the position of Lords of Gower and owned Oystermouth Castle for some time. They were not always popular with their tenants, and one complained about their behaviour to the king. The steward of Oystermouth Castle promptly kidnapped him and did not release him until he withdrew his allegations.

The 14th-century gatehouse was one of the last structures to be added to the castle. On each side, curved stone walls were clearly designed to form the inside walls of towers. What is not clear is whether the towers were ever even built or if they have been demolished and removed. The final addition to the medieval castle was 'Alina's Chapel', now accessible via steps and a modern walkway. In one of the arched recesses, the remains of contemporary fresco angels painted in red, yellow and black pigment can just be seen by those with a keen eye, hinting at how much more colourful the castle would have been in the past. More obvious is something that has also changed considerably since that time – the view across Swansea Bay.

Address Castle Road, Mumbles, SA3 4BA, www.swansea.gov.uk/oystermouthcastle |
Getting there Several buses to Oystermouth Square or Oystermouth Primary School;
limited parking in Oystermouth a few minutes' walk away | Hours See website for seasonal
hours | Tip Legend has it that a real family with the name Angel used to have a farmhouse
beyond Mumbles Head that was washed away by the flood of 1607. The land it stood on
was known as the Green Grounds.

77 Park Cwm Long Cairn

Meat off the bone

Around 6,000 years ago, hunter-gatherers lived in this part of what we now know as Wales. This was about 4,000 years after the last Ice Age. The ice had retreated, and the weather, which was warmer and wetter than ours, had provided ideal conditions for dense vegetation growth. Deer, pigs and wild cattle roamed the forests, providing plentiful food for Stone Age hunters.

This wedge-shaped cairn was used to bury the remains of up to 40 Stone Age men, women and children. It is thought that the community's dead were left in nearby Cathole Cave, to allow carnivorous animals to deflesh the bodies. The bones were then placed in the side chambers of the tomb. At that point, the chambers were up to 1.2 metres high and covered in stones – it was an impressive construction. Other finds from within the cairn include pottery, cremated bone, burnt flint and a large leaf-shaped arrowhead. Some animal bones have also been found, thought to have perhaps been scooped up from the floor of Cathole Cave along with the human ones.

At around this time, farming was introduced to Wales and soon became the primary means of feeding the population. This may have resulted in local families moving to an area more conducive to farming, as there was a period of hundreds of years when the cairn was not used. After this, bodies were placed in the central passageway instead of the side chambers, and they were not defleshed before being entombed.

Thousands of years later, after the Norman Invasion, the land around the cairn became the property of the de Breose family. They used it as a deer park. It is now known as Park Wood and houses one of the oldest forestry plantations in South Wales. Trees include oak, ash and sycamore, and the area is a Special Conservation Area. Somewhat ironically, there are now few deer on the Gower Peninsula, which gives the trees a good chance to thrive.

Address Parkmill, Swansea, SA3 2EH | Getting there Bus 112, 117 or 118 to Shepherds; parking at Gower Heritage Centre | Hours Accessible 24 hours | Tip From the car park, walk a short distance back towards Swansea to Shepherds if you fancy an ice cream.

78 Parc Howard Museum

Potty about Llanelly

South Wales might not be the first place you would look for an Italianate villa, but that is precisely what you will find on one of the hills overlooking Llanelli. The house was first known as Bryncaerau Mansion. When it was transformed into an Italianate-style building, the name was changed to Bryncaerau Castle. However, it was never a castle in anything but name. In 1911, the house was sold to Sir Edward Stafford Howard, a Liberal politician. The following year, on the first anniversary of his marriage to his second wife, Lady Stepney, he gifted the house to the council. The 999-year lease required that the house be used for the enjoyment of the public and that the gardens become a public park. This was when the house and gardens were renamed Parc Howard in his honour.

The commencement of the First World War temporarily scuppered plans for the house to be used for enjoyment. First, it housed Belgian refugees. Then, it was turned into a Red Cross auxiliary hospital for wounded servicemen. After the war, it was used as a rehabilitation centre for disabled soldiers, and it was only after that that it could be used as intended.

The park now houses delightful gardens and an unusual array of exotic trees. In 1962, Llanelli hosted the Eisteddfod, so the gardens are also home to a Gorsedd stone circle used for ceremonial events during the festival. The house is now a museum that holds the most extensive public collection of Llanelly pottery. The pottery was established by William Chambers, owner of Llanelly House, in 1839 and operated until 1921. It is particularly well known for its cockerel plates, most of which are thought to have been hand-painted by one person – Sarah Jane Roberts – despite the variable quality from plate to plate. The collection was owned by Lady Stepney and gifted to the town, along with the building in which to exhibit it.

Address Felinfoel Road, Llanelli, SA15 3LJ, www.cofgar.wales | Getting there Bus 128 to Parc Howard; train to Llanelli, then a two kilometre walk; on-street parking nearby | Hours Thu–Sun 10.30am–3.30pm, longer in summer (check website) | Tip Continue along the Felinfoel Road away from Llanelli for one kilometre to reach the Diplomat Hotel, a great place for refreshments.

79 Parkmill Watermill
Flour power

Feeling ground down? Imagine how you'd feel if you had to hand-grind your wheat or barley grain into flour. Using a quern stone, it would take four hours of turning for enough flour for one family-sized loaf of bread. On the other hand, this watermill can fill 40 sacks with flour in a day on just one of the two pairs of grinding stones. Although the flour is bagged in a modern, sterile room, it is assessed for grind quality by how the machinery sounds and how the meal feels when rubbed between the fingers.

You must be pretty savvy to run a successful business for 900 years. Here at Parkmill, Will the Mill and successive generations produced animal meal on the second pair of stones. The family adapted the wheel to run a sawmill as well, which helped to turn local trees into coffins far more efficiently than hand saws. As there are no protective guards on the blade of the circular saw, it's a good job it's disconnected now. Generations of Will the Mill's family are thought to have lost several fingers to the machinery – check out the photos in the mill cottage, and you will see lots of people hiding their hands in their sleeves and behind their backs.

Upstairs, a wood-turning lathe was set up on the mill, and Parkmill became home to a wheelwright, purportedly the best in South Wales. Later, another mill was built upstream to work a weaving shed. Further diversification happened during World War II when the Land Army was trained here to use the American tractors that were shipped over. This led to the maintenance of agricultural machinery as another strand to the family's bow.

It is said that the stream that powers the mill never runs dry, even in the worst of droughts. This could, at least in part, be because the flow from local springs is supplemented by water that flows underground naturally from the Brecon Beacons, roughly 100 kilometres (60 miles) away.

Address Gower Heritage Centre, Parkmill, Swansea, SA3 2EH, +44 (0)1792 371206, www.gowerheritagecentre.co.uk | Getting there Bus 112, 117 or 118 to Shepherds; car park on site, included in entrance fee | Hours Daily 10am–5pm | Tip There is a tearoom on site. If you prefer something stronger, the Gower Inn is a few hundred metres along the road to Swansea.

80 Penderyn Distillery
Bringing whisky home

On St David's Day in 2004, the first Welsh whisky produced in a century was launched. Why did it take so long for Wales to compete on the whisky-making stage? To understand that, you need to look back to the 19th century. Heading to the pub after a hard day's toil was in the Welsh DNA. However, as the country industrialised, a sociable evening started to morph into drunkenness for many, with all the associated consequences. In response, temperance societies sprang up nationwide, lobbying first for moderation, then abstinence, with some success. Drinking beer was often tolerated, but drinking spirits was not.

Despite this, a distillery opened in Frongoch in an attempt to challenge the Scottish and Irish whisky industries. In 1891, Queen Victoria visited, and in 1895, they received a royal warrant – Royal Welsh Whisky was born. It was not long lived. Seen as a curiosity outside Wales and hampered by the temperance movement at home, it closed in 1903.

By the start of the 21st century, temperance was no longer a strong influence, and Wales was importing a lot of whisky. It was time to try again, learning from past mistakes. The owners of Penderyn were determined to create a distinctive whisky that was highly regarded worldwide. They are unique in using a Faraday still and old madeira casks, resulting in a whisky with a clear identity. Their first distiller was tasked with creating a whisky that would achieve the highly-coveted International Wine and Spirits Competition Gold Medal. In 2018, Penderyn achieved that goal, sealing its international reputation. Despite a strong export market, the company retains its Welsh roots. All production and bottling takes place in Wales, and the company worked with other distilleries to establish protected UK GI status for Single Malt Welsh Whisky. This means that anyone using that name must do the same, protecting Welsh jobs.

Address Penderyn Swansea Copperworks Distillery, Hafod Copperworks, Landore, Swansea, SA1 2LQ, +44 (0)1792 381650, www.penderyn.wales, swansea@penderyn.wales | **Getting there** Bus 4, 4A or X6 to Landore; Landore Park & Ride | **Hours** See website for current information on visiting | **Tip** Despite its name, the Beer Park in Llanelli stocks a wide range of Penderyn whiskies including icons, the gold series and a couple of small batch whiskies. You can purchase bottles, drink in or buy online (www.beerpark.co.uk, SA14 8ND).

81 Penllergare Observatory
Pioneering photography

Could you imagine life without being able to take photographs outside? Without having seen a picture of a snowflake? Or the moon? Less than 200 years ago, photography was such a new science that no one had seen these things. And, without the work of John Dillwyn Llewelyn, his sister Mary and his daughter Thereza, we might not have done, either.

The Frenchman Louis Daguerre is credited with having invented photography, in 1839. Perhaps less well known is that, at around the same time, William Henry Fox Talbot worked out how to create photographs using a different chemical process. William was related to John Dillwyn Llewelyn, who built Penllergare Equatorial Observatory in the 1840s (he also created the gardens that contain Penllergare Waterfall). John, his sister and his daughter were fascinated with the possibilities of this new technology. In 1866, John devised a way of maintaining the integrity of photographic plates for several days, which enabled people to take photographs outside. This technology allowed his sister Mary's creative juices to flow. She soon became the first female photographer in Wales and is thought to have been the first person to capture someone smiling in a photograph. She was also the first person to photograph a snowman. John's daughter Thereza was the first person to take a photo of a snowflake.

John and Thereza also had a keen interest in astronomy, hence the construction of an observatory on his estate, and it was not long before they started to combine their two interests. In the 1850s, Penllergare Observatory was used by Thereza to take one of the first photos of the moon.

As such an important historical place, the observatory is undergoing restoration, with the aim of opening up a planetarium and exciting a whole new generation about astronomy and technology.

Address Penllergaer, Swansea, SA4 9GY | Getting there Bus 43, 56 or X13 Penllergaer Primary School or Penllergaer Roundabout; on-street parking nearby or Penllergare car park, SA4 9GS | Hours Viewable from the outside only | Tip Photographs taken by John Dillwyn Llewelyn can be seen, by appointment only, at the National Waterfront Museum, Swansea.

82 Penllergare Waterfalls

A polymath's paradise

John Dillwyn Llewelyn was one of those people who seemed to be good at everything. But then, he didn't need to spend time on trivial matters; his servants could do that for him. He was a fully paid-up member of the aristocracy and made the most of his connections to succeed at those things he loved doing. Two of those things were astronomy and science. The former led him to build an observatory on his inherited estate at Penllergare, and the latter led him to become a pioneering photographer.

Among his other interests was gardening; in his usual style, he excelled and became a nationally significant horticulturist. While at Penllergare, he transformed three kilometres of the Afon Llan Valley into a garden that combined wildness, innovation and domesticity. Exotic plants were status symbols in Victorian Britain, as many were newly discovered. Penllergare soon had a renowned collection, including rhododendrons and azaleas, bamboo, grapes and pineapples. A specimen monkey puzzle tree, also known as the Chilean pine, can still be seen in the gardens today. Although these things are commonplace today, they were cutting-edge imports at the time.

The gardens incorporated the growing of food, formal terraces leading down the side of the valley, and, very fashionably, a grotto. As part of the picturesque landscaping scheme, the river was dammed to create two lakes. The dam of the upper lake was designed to look like a natural waterfall and has three channels of water dropping over it. The waterfalls are probably the most photographed feature of the gardens, which are now managed by a charitable trust.

Looking closely, you may see a green chute built into the far bank. This is a micro hydro power generator installed in 2014. Given John Dillwyn Llewelyn's love of science, it seems like a fitting addition to the falls.

Address Penllergare Valley Woods, Penllergaer, Swansea, SA4 9GS, www.penllergare.org |
Getting there Bus 43, 56 or X13 Penllergaer Primary School or Penllergaer Roundabout;
parking on site | Hours Accessible 24 hours; parking daily 9am–6pm | Tip If a visit to the
gardens inspires you to upgrade your own, Pontarddulais Garden Centre is 4.5 kilometres
to the north.

83___Pennard Castle
Surrendered to sand

Ironically, Pennard Castle, built to defend against unwanted intruders, now has a bridle path running straight through the remains of its gatehouse. This gives everyone the right of access – even knights on horseback!

Pennard Castle was first built by the Normans in the 12th century. Following their successful invasion of England, the Normans were on the (slow) march through Wales. It took them over 200 years to triumph over the whole country – far longer than the handful of years it took to conquer England. However, it only took a few decades for them to assume control of the south of Wales to the Gower Peninsula. Initially, the castle was constructed from earthworks and timber, with a stone hall. It was not fortified with stone curtain walls and a gatehouse until the late 13th or early 14th century. The stone fortifications do not appear to have been very serious, perhaps because things were settling down between the Normans and the Welsh by then. They did not last for long either, but it was not Welsh insurgents who destroyed them.

Visiting the remains of the castle today, it appears to have been built on deep sand. That was not the case; it was actually built on a limestone spur. However, at some point in the 14th century, the castle and surrounding settlement, including a church, were swamped by sand and abandoned, much like the castle at Kenfig. By that point, the whole of Wales was under the control of the Normans and the land was peaceful, so maybe the owners surrendered in their battle against the sand as the castle was not likely to be needed for defensive purposes again.

Nevertheless, it must have been galling to give up a home in such a splendid location. Today, it is a great place to visit for its views over Pennard Pill winding across the bottom of the valley, Three Cliffs Bay, and Oxwich Bay to Oxwich Point.

Address Across Pennard Golf Club, Southgate Road, Southgate, Swansea, SA3 2BT |
Getting there Bus 14 to Southgate Post Office; limited on-street parking nearby. Walk on
public paths across the golf course to access the castle, which lies NW of the clubhouse |
Hours Accessible 24 hours | Tip The Southgate is a popular pub a few minutes' walk from
the golf clubhouse.

84 Phil Bennett Statue

A giant statue for a giant of a man

Phil Bennett was a giant. Not literally, of course. In fact, at 1.7 metres tall, he would look rather short in a rugby line-up today. He was a giant in the world of rugby though, fully deserving of this giant statue in his home village of Felinfoel.

Phil first played rugby for Felinfoel RFC, but it was not long before he was snapped up by Llanelli RFC, also known as the Scarlets. Loyal to his local area, he lived in Felinfoel for the rest of his life and played for the Scarlets until he retired. He played 414 matches for them in total, during which he landed 131 tries and scored over 2,500 points. The people of Llanelli remain proud of the Scarlets' win over the New Zealand All Blacks in 1972, a match in which Phil Bennett played.

This was a man who was destined for greater things than local rugby. He played 29 times for Wales. He was a member of the British and Irish Lions team when they toured South Africa in 1974 and won 21 out of 22 matches, drawing the other. He captained the team for their 1977 tour of New Zealand. He also sometimes played for the Barbarians, an invitational team of players hand-picked from clubs around the world. In 1978, he was honoured with an OBE for his services to rugby football. Not only does he feature in the Wales Sports Hall of Fame, but also in the World Rugby Hall of Fame.

Phil Bennett was also a giant off the pitch. When he no longer played, his love of rugby continued to shine through his commentary on the BBC. He was well-loved locally as a humble, kind and caring man who saved any ferocity for his time on the pitch. This statue, hewn by Simon Hedger, was unveiled just a few short months before Phil's death. During the unveiling, he was keen to tell everyone that he had also played for Felinfoel. After his death, the Welsh Rugby Union said he was 'a Welsh rugby legend in every sense and true gentleman'.

Address Opposite Holy Trinity Church, Felinfoel, Llanelli, SA14 8BH | Getting there Bus 128 to Royal Oak or L 2 to Co-op; on-street parking nearby | Hours Accessible 24 hours | Tip The Scarlets play at the Parc y Scarlets Stadium at Parc Pemberton.

85   Rhossili Sunflowers
Nothing is quite as it seems

The Vile at Rhossili is anything but! It is the strip of farmland atop a narrow peninsula on the edge of the Gower Area of Outstanding Natural Beauty. From one side, the three golden miles of Rhossili Bay sweep to the north, backed by Rhossili Down. From the other, the Bristol Channel reaches across to the distant Devon coastline. To the west, Worm's Head dominates, the tidal island famed for its natural arch, blow hole and seals basking on the rocks. The name 'Worm' derives from a Viking word meaning dragon or serpent because they thought the rocks looked like a dragon rising from the deep – a somewhat more romantic notion than that of an earthworm!

The Vile is mainly owned by the National Trust and has been returned to medieval field management patterns of a patchwork of different-sized strips. The crops grown are mostly chosen now for their attractiveness to wildlife rather than human palates. Wildflowers grow abundantly, and the area is abuzz with insects during spring and summer.

Continue to walk among the wild ponies towards Worm's Head in July and August, and there is now an additional attraction – eight acres of fields planted with 400,000 sunflowers. A veritable cornucopia of blooms awaits, a sea of yellow to bathe in, punctuated by a white flower here and a deep red one there – even the sunflowers are not all the colour you would expect! Wander through the field and watch their faces as they follow the sun from east to west. Listen to the bees buzzing in delight as they drink the sweet nectar. Stay into the evening, and you might be treated to a spectacular ocean sunset. The sunflower fields are, understandably, a popular choice for romantic proposals, wedding photographs and social media posts. And if you prefer to take something more tangible than photographs home with you, you can even pick a few stems of your own.

Address Rhossili, SA3 1PR, +44 (0)1792 335793, www.rhossilisunflowers.co.uk, info@rhossilisunflowers.co.uk | Getting there Bus 118 or 119 to Rhossili; parking at National Trust Rhossili car park | Hours Sunflowers usually mid July – early Sept; check website for opening hours | Tip Rhossili Bay is a popular surfing beach and great for a stroll. Look out for the skeleton of the *Helvetia* shipwreck sticking out from the sand.

86 Roman Bridge
A tale of two halves

The Romans arrived in Britain in 55 B.C. and started conquering the island about 90 years later. From A.D. 49 to A.D. 74, they fought the tribes in South Wales, often collectively called the Silures, as they slowly made their way across the country. Forts were built at intervals of one day's march apart, from Caerleon on the northern edge of Newport heading west. These fort locations included Neath, Loughor, Carmarthen and Llandovery, apparently bypassing Swansea.

Despite significant research, we still do not know the location of all Roman roads and forts. In 2018, during a particularly dry summer, the Royal Commission on the Ancient and Historical Monuments of Wales organised flights across the country and found what looked like a hitherto unknown Roman road heading south from Carmarthen. This raised the question of whether there was also a Roman fort at Kidwelly. Fragments of mosaic flooring indicated that there was a significant Roman villa or military building in Mumbles. If the Romans had travelled from the fort at Neath, they would have needed to cross the Blackpill River at some point, so it is possible that there was once a Roman bridge here.

It seems likely that, 500 years after the Romans left, this became an important crossing point for the Normans travelling between their castles at Swansea and Oystermouth. However, the first written record of a bridge here dates from the late 17th century when surveyors for the Oystermouth Leet Court (a form of manorial court) noted the need for repairs. This was tricky, as the river marks the historic boundary between the parishes of Swansea and Oystermouth, and each party was only willing to repair their half. Some five years later, the Oystermouth side still needed attention. Whether or not that was the same bridge we see today, this one is known to be at least 200 years old and was repaired in 2015.

Address Blackpill, Sketty, SA3 5AX | Getting there Several buses to Blackpill Lido; nearest car park Clyne Gardens | Hours Unrestricted | Tip Fragments of the Roman mosaic floor found when extending All Saints Church in Mumbles can be seen in the west corner of the south aisle.

87 Sauna on the Beach
A portal to relaxation

Imagine stepping into a world of warmth and tranquillity, where the stresses of daily life melt away and your body and mind are rejuvenated. This is the allure of the sauna, a time-honoured tradition that offers a host of potential health benefits. The warmth of a sauna causes pores to open and sweat to form. Many believe this allows dead skin cells and bacteria to be rinsed away and toxins to be expelled from the body. The heat can relax sore muscles, aiding recovery from injury or exertion. Some also consider the transition from hot to cold and back again to give health benefits. There is not much good quality medical evidence around these benefits yet. Still, there is no doubt that many people find saunas enjoyable and relaxing, and the contrast between hot and cold invigorating.

Ty Sawna on Oxwich Beach takes the sauna experience to a whole new level by immersing visitors in the beautiful surroundings of the bay. The half-moon windows offer gorgeous views of the sandy beach and breaking waves. The opportunity to plunge into the bay or drench yourself with a bucket of seawater adds an extra dimension to the hot-cold contrast, enhancing the therapeutic effects of the sauna. Beyond the physical benefits, Ty Sawna also offers an opportunity for social connection and camaraderie in this device-free space. With room for up to eight people in each of the two saunas, you can either enjoy the experience with friends or join one of the communal sessions.

Whether basking in the golden glow of a sunset, bathing in the ethereal light of the moon or admiring the sparkle of a frost-covered beach from the heat of your seat, the benefits of a sauna on the beach are bound to linger long after the warmth has dissipated. As with any new experience, it's always wise to listen to your body and consult a healthcare professional if you have any concerns about your safety.

Address Bay Beach, Oxwich, SA3 1LS, +44 (0)7933 806546, www.tysawna.co.uk, tysawna@gmail.com | Getting there Bus 117 to Oxwich Cross; parking adjacent to beach | Hours By appointment only | Tip Gower Coast Adventures operates from Oxwich Bay over the summer months, and customers often see seals and dolphins on their trips around the coastline (www.gowercoastadventures.co.uk).

88 Singleton Boating Lake
Leonardo's pedaloes

As far as we know, Leonardo da Vinci never visited Swansea. However, his legacy lives on in an unexpected way on Singleton Boating Lake, as it was da Vinci who first envisaged and drew a pedal-powered boat, in the 15th century. His boat was driven by a hand crank, turning a much larger paddle wheel. This indicated his understanding of how using different-sized wheels with cogs could affect gearing. However, he was either unaware of or had forgotten about the law of leverage described by Archimedes over 1,500 years earlier. For a small hand crank to turn a large wheel fast through water requires more force than a human arm is capable of delivering. All the power for such a design comes from the muscles in the arms and back, which are far weaker than the leg muscles. Maybe that is why today's pedaloes are powered by the legs, although they are still not terribly efficient. That might explain why they are only used for recreational purposes, to enable people to enjoy the tranquillity of a pootle around lakes like this one at the edge of Singleton Park, rather than for speed or efficiency.

Leonardo da Vinci was a prolific scientist and artist who was also meticulous in his observations and drawings. His curiosity drove him to question the reasons behind everything he saw. If there was a pattern behind, for example, the behaviour of water flowing around obstructions, he realised there must be 'rules' that applied to those circumstances and tried to work out what they were. His work has provided the foundation for many of our scientific quests since.

How would da Vinci's artistic and scientific sensibilities react to the gaudy colours and plastic moulding of the pedaloes on the lake? Would he be thrilled to see his invention in use? Curious about how this new material was created? Or horrified at the lack of sophistication? Sadly, no one will ever know.

Address Mumbles Road, Sketty, SA3 5AU, www.swansea.gov.uk/singletonboatinglake |
Getting there Several buses to Boating Lake or Sketty Lane; parking in University or
Foreshore car parks | Hours See website for seasonal hours | Tip The popular Pub on the
Pond next to the lake is family and dog friendly.

89 Singleton Botanical Gardens

Hothouse Flowers

In the northern reaches of Singleton Park, the open parkland landscape transforms into far more intimate spaces. This is Singleton Botanical Gardens. Over 100 years ago, the council bought these gardens from the Vivian family, who owned the Hafod Copperworks. The Vivians were well known for the quality of their kitchen produce, including rare and exotic fruits such as pineapples and peaches.

In 1926, what we now know as the Botanical Gardens was opened as the Education Garden. For a few years during World War II, the gardens were used as part of the Dig for Victory campaign to grow food that it was no longer possible to import. Around 1,500 American troops were billeted in Singleton Park for the D-Day landings, so the food produced in the Botanical Gardens next door would also have been a vital part of their diet – and a factor in the campaign's success. After the war, the gardens continued to be used as a public park, but by the late 1980s, the wooden glasshouses had become unsafe. They were replaced by the glasshouses that we see today.

The path in the temperate house meanders through, under and beside a riot of greenery, including palms, ferns, orchids, hibiscus and insectivorous plants, and past a pond with a small waterfall and a curtain of flowers suspended over the water. This is a fantastic place to visit on a cold and wet day. The exotic theme continues outside the glasshouses with formal beds containing cactuses and other tropical plants that are hardy enough to live through our winters.

In 1991, the garden was renamed the Singleton Botanical Gardens. A few years later, the Friends of the City of Swansea Botanical Complex was founded to support the maintenance and development of this and other gardens within the city. The volunteers remain active in the gardens, and run a shop on the site to raise funds for its maintenance.

Address Singleton Park, Sketty, Swansea, SA2 8PW, www.swansea.gov.uk | Getting there Several buses go to Parc Beck, then a 0.5 kilometre walk; on-street parking on Brynmill Lane, then a 0.5 kilometre walk | Hours From 10am; closing time dependent on season | Tip The Botanical Gardens are part of Singleton Park, a large open parkland with areas of garden, perfect for a stroll or picnic.

90 Sjømanns Kirken

From pit props to pulpit

The growing number and size of coal mines in South Wales in the 18th century created an increased demand for wood that could be used as pit props. By the 19th century, no local supplies remained, and timber had to be imported for this purpose. Scandinavia was producing plenty of wood for export and needed coal. This led to a growing number of Scandinavian ships visiting Swansea, arriving with timber and leaving with coal, and each had a complement of Scandinavian seafarers. In the 1890s, the Norwegian church in Bergen decided to support those Scandinavian mariners by opening a church and mission on the dock at Newport. Over the next 20 years or so, the trade with Newport declined, and the church was dismantled and rebuilt at the entrance to the dock in Swansea. The small building contained both a church and a mission.

For several decades, the Norwegian church thrived in Swansea, but by the second half of the 20th century, the port in Swansea was declining, and the church in Bergen decided it was time to close their outreach here. However, a Norwegian who had settled in Swansea asked for permission to run the church as a lay preacher alongside the local Norwegian community. This arrangement continued for 32 years, and the church was not shut down until 1998, around 100 years after it had first opened in Newport.

By this time, the redevelopment of Swansea docks into what is now the Maritime Quarter had begun. In 2004, the Norwegian church was dismantled, renovated and re-erected in its current position. Having been deconsecrated, the building was available for alternative uses, and currently houses a children's nursery.

Sjømanns Kirken continues to support Norwegians living, working or travelling outside Norway. They currently operate 28 churches and have chaplains in around 80 countries. They also visit Norwegian ships and oil rigs in the North Sea.

Address Langdon Road, Swansea, SA1 8AG | Getting there Several buses go to Cape Horner; nearest parking at Parc Tawe Retail Park, SA1 2AL | Hours Viewable from the outside only | Tip The area around the church has many waterside cafés and restaurants.

91 St Helen's Ground
First, fastest, finest

Wales has a glittering sporting history, strongly supported by players from this area who represented local teams at St Helen's. During Swansea's industrial heyday in the 18th century, Swansea Cricket Club bought this land, levelled it and covered it in turf. The ground enjoyed its own cricketing heyday in the 1960s when Glamorgan Cricket Club twice beat the Australian country team here. In 1968, the world's first score of six sixes in one over was achieved here, and almost a decade later St Helen's was home to the world's first double century on record.

The ground has not limited itself to cricketing firsts, though. It is also where the first Welsh home international was held for rugby. Sadly, the Wales team failed to score against England, who claimed seven goals, one drop goal and six tries – the equivalent 82 – 0 using today's scoring.

The Welsh team did not simply accept defeat, though, and has made up for it many times since, keeping a close tally against its much larger neighbour. St Helen's ground was used for international men's rugby matches until 1954, when Cardiff Arms Park was deemed more suited to the larger crowds. More recently, it has also hosted the international women's game.

At a club level, St Helen's is home to Swansea Rugby Football Club, which itself has an illustrious history. The 'All Whites' defeated Australia (the Wallabies) in 1908 and South Africa (the Springboks) in 1912. When they beat New Zealand (the All Blacks) in 1935, they were the first club side to achieve that feat – and also to have beaten the 'Big 3' teams of the southern hemisphere.

Sporting success pumps through the arteries of the Welsh nation, and the St Helen's stadium has been at the heart of it. And although this ground has been largely superseded for international fixtures, it retains its importance in the annals of Welsh sporting history.

Address Bryn Road, Swansea, SA2 0AR, www.swansearfc.co.uk | **Getting there** Several buses to St Helen's Cricket Ground | **Hours** See website for current information on visiting | **Tip** If you prefer your sport more staid, there's a lawn bowling green nearby in Victoria Park (www.swanseaba.com).

92 St Mary Virgin, Rhossili

The coolest stained-glass window

For a church that's over 800 years old, St Mary's in Rhossili sports a very modern stained-glass window. In cool blue and white hues, it depicts two people standing on the edge of a crevasse. The scene is bleak and stark, not unlike the conditions that Captain Scott's expedition faced on their deadly exploration of the Antarctic. And that is no coincidence.

Scott had been to the Antarctic before, but this time, he wanted to claim the South Pole for Britain. He did not realise that the Norwegian explorer Roald Amundsen was trying to do precisely the same thing for Norway. After six weeks of crossing the ice, Scott's team found the South Pole – with a Norwegian flag already firmly planted. They had lost the race they didn't know they were in by about a month.

Of course, there was no airport back then at the South Pole, so, dejected and exhausted, they started their return trip across the icy continent. Among their number was Edgar Evans, who was born at Middleton Hall Cottage at Rhossili. As a young lad, he had been enchanted by stories of derring-do at sea, spurred partly by seeing the wreck of the *Helvetia* on Rhossili Beach (now just a few wooden ribs sticking up from the sand). He signed up to join the navy as soon as he turned 15, where he met Scott. He was part of the team that conducted the first, successful, expedition to Antarctica, and married his sweetheart in this church on his return.

A month after reaching the South Pole, Edgar Evans collapsed on the return journey. He was suffering from malnutrition, frostbite and a deep cut to his hand and died later that day. The remaining team members continued for another few weeks before they, too, were scuppered by the conditions. They were eventually found some eight months later, only 11 miles from a supply depot where they could have restocked with essential, life-saving goods, had they managed to reach it.

Address St Mary Virgin, Rhossili, Swansea, SA3 1PN, www.churchinwales.org.uk | Getting there Bus 118 to Rhossili; park at National Trust Worms Head car park, SA3 1PR | Hours Daily 10am–3.30pm | Tip There is a blue plaque commemorating Edgar Evans on Middleton Hall Cottage. Head towards Swansea on the B4247 and turn left onto Bunker's Hill.

93__Stradey Park Memorial

Who beat the All Blacks?

On a dull October day in 2022, one of the conference rooms at Parc y Scarlets rugby ground was full of people celebrating the launch of the Welsh-language version of the children's book *'Gwylia!'* (Watch Out!), designed to help children stay safe. Children from a local school were on a low stage, singing *'Sosban Fach'*, an old Welsh folk song about saucepans.

Zinzan Brook, the former New Zealand All Blacks rugby forward, was helping to promote the book. At almost two metres tall, he towered above most of the others there, even while sitting. One of the children sang a bum note, starting a new verse before his classmates. He looked mortified, but Zinzan gave him a thumbs up, and the boy visibly relaxed. Seconds later, without missing a beat, the choir switched from Welsh to English and chanted 'Who beat the All Blacks?' before continuing their song in Welsh.

The audience laughed. Thankfully, Zinzan Brook laughed, too. Over 50 years earlier, the Scarlets, the Llanelli club side, had beaten the All Blacks, and many in the town are still proud of their achievement. Llanelli has a pub named after Carwyn James, the team's coach. It is painted scarlet and has the score proudly displayed on each side of the front door. People still talk about how it felt being in the crowd and the atmosphere in the town after the match. And why not? After all, the All Blacks are a pretty unassailable team. They have an almost unblemished history against the Welsh national team (92% wins) and beat England nearly 80% of the time. Only one national team in the world comes close to matching them, and that is South Africa.

The Stradey Park stadium is where all that excitement happened. It was a sad day for many when the new Parc y Scarlets was built, and Stradey Park was demolished. It seems fitting that there is, at least, a memorial stone to Llanelli's proud sporting history.

1879 - 2008

PARC Y STRADE

In almost 130 years Llanelli RFC fielded
Over 5000 players
192 Internationals
2 British and Irish Lions coaches
24 British and Irish Lions

With thanks to
Llanelli Rural Council
Abbey Masonry & Restoration Ltd
Phil Bowen Paving Ltd
Taylor Wimpey PLC
WRW Group Ltd
Dyfed Steels Ltd
Designed by
Roger Lewis

Address Stryd Bennett, Llanelli, SA15 4DQ | **Getting there** X11 bus to Maesycoed,
Llanelli; on-street parking nearby | **Hours** Unrestricted | **Tip** One of the most popular
chippies in Llanelli, Queens Fish & Chips, is on Maes Y Coed between the memorial
and the main road.

94 Swansea Arena Roof Garden
A dazzling display

By day, this extensive rooftop garden resounds with the gleeful cries of children playing. They are fascinated by the hand-powered water pump that creates a stream down a gentle slope lined with granite cobbles, and they love to run around and over the other garden structures. Older children and adults get competitive around the table tennis, while those with less energy relax in the café and enjoy the view. Drought- and wind-tolerant grasses and trees soften the edges of the paths and provide food and shelter for wildlife.

The garden stands five metres above the street, as it was once part of the infrastructure that allowed coal to be dropped into freighters berthed in the dock. It's hard to imagine this area as a busy port now, with a fine view over the homes, restaurants, marina and Meridian Tower. The curvaceous, molten-copper-coloured walls of Swansea Arena rise above one end of the garden, adding structure and colour.

By night, the garden is transformed as it throngs with concertgoers. The 9,800-square-metre arena seats 3,500 for concerts and 2,196 for theatre and has attracted acts such as Frankie Boyle, Orchestral Manoeuvres in the Dark, Paloma Faith and Strictly Come Dancing The Professionals. At dusk, the arena's golden walls morph into the UK's largest digital façade. Over 100,000 individually programmable LED lights are built into the corrugated aluminium panels that wrap around the whole building, enabling dazzling light shows that are visible from all directions.

The Swansea Arena development is part of a billion-pound programme to regenerate Swansea City Centre. The arena and the bridge over the busy Oystermouth Road are part of Copr Bay, which links the city with the Maritime Quarter and the bay, and will also include a hotel, homes, offices and restaurants.

Address Oystermouth Road, Maritime Quarter, Bae Copr Bay, Swansea, SA1 3BX |
Getting there Bus to Swansea Bus Station; train to Swansea, then a one kilometre walk |
Hours Accessible 24 hours | Tip If you like music, check out the annual Escape Festival
held in Singleton Park over the summer.

95 Swansea Castle
Quay to the city's success

During the post-World War II rebuilding of Swansea city centre, Swansea Castle was dwarfed by tower blocks and buildings, some of which King Charles III might understandably consider to be 'monstrous carbuncles', but it remains the foundation stone upon which this city was built.

Before the Normans arrived, a small settlement probably existed near the River Tawe, taking advantage of the natural resources and strategic location that would later prove crucial to Swansea's development. When the Norman rulers built a castle to protect the river crossing, it toppled over a whole row of dominoes that led to Swansea's industrial success. The castle needed a means of re-supply, so a quay was built on the west bank of the River Tawe, which ran closer to the castle than it does today.

The quay provided the basis of a trading port between the navigable river and the bay that provided a safe anchorage for ships. This put Swansea in pole position to export the coal that was found in abundance nearby. Coal was needed to heat the great furnaces of the Industrial Revolution. Swansea's trading advantage was so great that it also became easier to transport ore into Wales here rather than exporting the coal to the ore. Thus began the industrial development of the Swansea area and the birth of the Industrial Revolution.

The castle was not used for military purposes after Edward I's conquest of Wales in the late 13th century – neither Owain Glyndŵr's rebellion at the turn of the 15th century nor the Civil War of the 17th touched it. Time, however, took its toll, as the building was used for diverse activities, including copper smelting, glass manufacturing, imprisoning debtors, housing the poor and, indeed, housing the rich. What remains offers only glimpses of its former glory, but that does not in any way reduce the importance of the place in the city's history.

Address 8 Castle Street, Swansea, SA1 1DW, www.swansea.gov.uk/swanseacastle | Getting there Bus 16 to Castle Square; nearest car park Worcester Place | Hours Unrestricted | Tip The oldest pub in Swansea is close to the castle. Head about 50 metres down Princess Way from Castle Square and The Olde Cross Keys is on the left (12 St Mary's Street).

96 Swansea Community Farm

The only city farm in Wales

Swansea Community Farm is a small working farm determined to make a big difference. Producing food, including meat, eggs, honey, fruit and vegetables, is an essential part of its remit. This is not a place for children to visit and pet the animals (although that might be possible under supervision) but to learn about where their food comes from and how it is produced. Visitors are welcome to walk around. They can admire the livestock and productive growing areas, all managed by local volunteers, and buy some supplies in the shop. There's a firepit and picnic table for visitors to use, too.

In addition to producing food, the farm provides a home to rare breeds to help maintain genetic diversity in the stock of farm animals. As many are Welsh breeds, it is also protecting Welsh cultural heritage.

The volunteers benefit immensely from working on the farm, as all five 'pillars of wellbeing' are achieved: connecting with others, physical activity, learning new skills, giving to others and spending time in the moment, noticing nature.

The final strand of the farm's mission is to provide environmental conservation services using its animals. The donkeys browse the neighbouring Cadle Heath Local Nature Reserve to keep shrubs from taking over. The farm is also working on a 'Goatbusters' project, where the goats are involved in conservation grazing. Meat and dairy production are often considered environmentally damaging; feeding goats on land that would benefit from grazing and using their milk and meat is one sustainable alternative to standard models.

Visitors to the farm are reminded of the inextricable links between the land, our food and our communities. In a world increasingly disconnected from its agricultural roots, Swansea Community Farm provides a vital bridge between the three.

Address 2 Pontardulais Road, Cadle, Fforest-fach, SA5 4BA, +44 (0)1792 578384, www.swanseacommunityfarm.org.uk, info@swanseacommunityfarm.org.uk | Getting there Several buses to Ivorites or Ivorites Arms; limited parking on site | Hours General visitors Tue, Thu & Sat 10am – 4pm, groups by appointment | Tip The farm shop in Dunvant stocks a wide range of locally grown and produced food in their shop and café (Facebook @Farm Shop Dunvant).

97 Swansea Footgolf
Bend it like Woosnam

Once upon a time, a golf course was squeezed between Mumbles Road and the beach at Blackpill. These days, you are unlikely to see men wearing garish plus fours, with caddies carrying their clubs across the course. Instead, you are more likely to see family groups or students in their everyday garb, kicking footballs. This is one of the things that makes this footgolf site so popular. Elsewhere, many footgolf courses are on golf courses, and similar formal rules apply about attire and behaviour. Here, the footgolf course has replaced the golf course, and it is all about having fun, whether you are wearing football kit, jeans or a sparkly tiara.

The clubhouse is a little basic; it's an early air raid warning shelter left over from World War II, with a picnic bench under cover outside. But the course should not be judged on the quality of the clubhouse. There are 18 holes here, with fairways and greens, just like a golf course. The holes are a little larger to fit a football, and the greens are cut longer to slow the ball down. On 'proper' golf courses, you occasionally see a ball kicked out of the rough and back onto the course. Here, that is the whole idea – not something you do furtively, hoping that nobody spots you cheating!

Although not taken too seriously by most, footgolf has developed into a sport with its own World Cup, and some of the Wales team play here on this course. Footgolf is not yet a professional sport, but you might get lucky and spot one of the local football professionals kicking a ball around here, too. There is talk about proposing footgolf as an Olympic sport. That possibility might be fanciful or – at the very least – some way into the future. For now, for most people, it's just a fun thing to do on a sunny afternoon with a group of friends. So why not grab a pair of trainers and some mates and head down to the seashore together for a bit of a kickabout and a laugh?

Address Mumbles Road, Blackpill, Swansea, SA3 5AU, +44 (0)1792 207544, www.futuregolfventures.com, info@swanseafootgolf.com | Getting there Several buses go to Ashleigh Road; park at Blackpill car park, SA3 5AT | Hours Apr – Oct Mon – Fri 11am – 6pm, Sat & Sun 10am – 6pm | Tip The Woodman pub, a short walk to the south, is a popular place to grab a meal with family or friends.

98 Swansea Jack Memorial

Celebrating the Dog of the Century

What comes to mind when you think of people doing weird and wonderful things to raise money for charity? Running a marathon dressed as a camel, perhaps? Sitting in a bath of baked beans? Or maybe a parachute jump? Plenty of people have thrown themselves out of perfectly good aeroplanes as a fundraising stunt, but what about throwing yourself out of a perfectly good boat to be rescued by a dog? That's what the Newfound Friends of Bristol organises for those brave (or foolhardy) enough to give it a go. Participants are given life jackets to wear, and the dogs undergo rigorous training, learning to tow people to safety using specially designed harnesses.

Back in the 1930s, no such health and safety considerations were in place, and people seemed to have a fondness for getting into trouble in Swansea docks. Between 1931 and 1937, one dog is reputed to have rescued as many as 27 drowning people and two floundering dogs from the water. Swansea Jack's heroic deeds quickly made him a local celebrity, and it was not long before he started winning awards for his actions. The first was a silver collar, awarded to him by Swansea Council after he rescued a swimmer in trouble. Later, he received two bronze medals from the National Canine Defence League (now the Dogs Trust), the dog's equivalent of the Victoria Cross. He was awarded 'Bravest Dog of the Year' by a national newspaper in 1936 and, more recently, 'Dog of the Century' by the Newfound Friends of Bristol.

The nickname 'Swansea Jack' is used to refer to people from Swansea, and Swansea City Football Club fans are known as 'The Jacks'. Some like to think that the name came from the exploits of this heroic dog, but it seems more likely that it is because sailors were known as 'Jacks'. Either way, the dog's name lives on at football matches, in a children's book depicting his adventures and on this seafront memorial.

ERECTED TO THE MEMORY OF
SWANSEA JACK
THE BRAVE RETRIEVER WHO SAVED 27 HUMAN
AND 2 CANINE LIVES FROM DROWNING.
LOVED AND MOURNED BY ALL DOG LOVERS
DIED OCTOBER 2ND 1937 AT THE AGE OF 7 YEARS
"NE'ER HAD MANKIND MORE FAITHFUL FRIEND THAN THOU
WHO OFT THY LIFE DIDST LEND TO SAVE SOME HUMAN
SOUL FROM DEATH"
OWNER-TRAINER W.M.THOMAS

Address Mumbles Road, Brynmill, SA2 0AY | Getting there Several buses to St Helen's
Cricket Ground or Recreation Ground; nearest car park Recreation Ground | Hours
Unrestricted | Tip Human heroes are commemorated at the cenotaph, a five-minute walk
west along the front.

99 _ Swansea Little Theatre

Small in name, grand in stature

In 2024, Swansea Little Theatre celebrated its centenary. When it was established, Swansea was a small provincial town rather than the cosmopolitan city it is today, with what we would now consider poor transport links to the rest of the country. Swansea Little Theatre provided ordinary Swansea folk with access to productions they otherwise would not have had – an evening at a play in London's West End would have been a rare treat for a privileged few.

Swansea Little Theatre started life staging six shows a year in a church hall in Mumbles' Southend. In the 1950s, it resided at the Palace Theatre, where Sir Anthony Hopkins made his debut stage performance in its production of 'Have a Cigarette'. In the 1970s, the council offered the theatre company a derelict car showroom on the as-yet undeveloped South Dock. It must have taken some vision to see the potential of the building. Volunteers had to contend with the rubbish left by the previous occupants, a leaking roof and the building's new four-legged residents as they renovated it and converted it into a theatre. The building was named after Dylan Thomas, a one-time company member and long-term committee member. It opened its doors in 1979. In 1983, shortly after the dock had been redeveloped, it was officially opened by another local legend, Sir Harry Secombe.

The theatre company continues to stage six varied shows a year, as well as providing space for visiting comedians, music festivals and touring companies. The building is totally wheelchair accessible for the audience and performers, enabling a wide range of entertainers to 'tread the boards'.

In addition, Theatr Na n'Og hires the space for three months a year. During this time, it provides theatrical education to thousands of children. Beyond a doubt, the Swansea Little Theatre might be small in name, but is grand in stature.

Address Dylan Thomas Theatre, Gloucester Place, Maritime Quarter, Swansea, SA1 1TY, +44 (0)1792 473238, www.dylanthomastheatre.org.uk, info@dylanthomastheatre.org.uk | Getting there Bus 7 to Burrows Place; several car parks nearby | Hours See website for current information on visiting | Tip The square in front of the theatre is a lovely place to soak up the vibes of the area, and there are several eateries on the waterfront for a pre-theatre dinner.

100 Swansea Museum Façade

Keeping things in perspective

Established during the reign of Queen Victoria, Swansea Museum was born out of the era's fascination with science, natural history and the arts. It is the oldest museum in Wales, built from stone in 1841 in the neo-classical style. It is an elegant building that, luckily, survived Swansea's Blitz in February 1941, which destroyed many other historic buildings in the city. The door and windows in the façade are tall and impressive, but they are not necessarily as tall as they seem.

It is thought that the Romans understood the laws of linear perspective, but no records remained after the fall of the Roman Empire. It was not until the 15th century that they were rediscovered, again by an Italian. Filippo Brunelleschi was a Renaissance architect who was dissatisfied with how buildings were depicted. He set his prodigious mind to the question and worked out that you can give the impression of depth on a flat surface by converging parallel lines to a vanishing point on the horizon. He turned this realisation into a mathematical scale, which meant that artists and architects could calculate measurements and accurately represent buildings on the page.

By 1841, these rules were well used and understood, including by the architect who designed Swansea Museum. Looking carefully, it is possible to see that the stone on each side of the door and windows is wider at the top than at the bottom. That means the door and windows are narrower at the top than at the bottom – the difference is not just a matter of perspective and distance. By subtly tapering the door and windows, the architect created an optical illusion that makes the building appear taller and more imposing than it actually is.

The museum is full of fascinating artefacts from around the world, including an Egyptian mummy from 200 B.C. and a painted feather postcard from 1898.

Address Victoria Road, Maritime Quarter, Swansea, SA1 1SN, +44 (0)1792 653763, www.swanseamuseum.co.uk, museum.swansea@swansea.gov.uk | Getting there Several buses to Sainsbury's Quay Parade; nearest car park Swansea City Gates | Hours Façade unrestricted; museum Tue–Sun & Bank Holiday Mondays 10.30am–4.30pm | Tip Museum Park is home to the annual Waterfront Winterland funfair, ferris wheel and ice rink from mid-November to early January (https://swanseawaterfrontwinterland.cymru).

101 Swansea Observatory
Ready for blast-off

It can't be a coincidence that the observatory on the seafront in the Maritime Quarter looks like a space rocket propped up on its launch pad at Kennedy Space Center. It wouldn't be too much of a stretch of the imagination to be standing on West Pier, waiting with bated breath for the launch countdown to begin. Ten, nine, eight, seven…

In reality, people always needed their imagination to travel to the stars from here. When it was first built in the early 1990s, the observatory did house a telescope – the largest optical astronomical telescope in Wales – so the stars seemed much closer to those looking through it. At that time, the observatory was home to the Swansea Astronomical Society. The society wanted somewhere near the city to entice the public to learn more about the universe and enjoy the wonders of the night sky. It would throw monthly 'star parties' and hold exhibitions on the ground floor of the building. It vacated the building in 2010 after a disagreement with Swansea City Council (the landlord), and moved its observatory to the airport. In its new home, the skies do not suffer from as much light pollution from the city, so are much darker – and therefore easier to see the stars in.

The Observatory is not, however, going to waste, and you can still hold a party here. After many years spent on renovations, this is a stunning place to grab a bite to eat or celebrate a special occasion. As you enter the restaurant, a panoramic view opens up across Swansea Bay. On a sunny day, the water sparkles like sequins in the breeze, rivalling the beauty of any starry night. As darkness falls, the bay becomes a dark and moody expanse, sometimes reflecting the ethereal silver glow of the moon. It may not be possible to see the stars up close, but step out onto the deck on a clear night, and they are still there to enjoy in all their glory.

Address Marine Promenade, Swansea, SA1 1YB, +44 (0)1792 960526, www.facebook.com/
swanseaobservatory | Getting there Bus 7 to Marriott Hotel; park at Paxton Street car park,
SA1 | Hours Viewable from the outside only; restaurant daily 10am–10pm | Tip If you
head east from The Observatory to the Paxton Street car park, you will find a children's play
area and a boardwalk over the dunes.

102 Swiss Cottage

Live so that you may live again

Building an Alpine-style cottage in your garden was the thing to do for the British upper classes in the early 19th century. This example was designed by Peter Frederick Robinson for the Vivian family's garden. Having founded the Hafod Copperworks, which became the largest in the world, the Vivians profited well from the Industrial Revolution in Swansea. Commissioning a garden building designed by a well-known London architect strongly indicated their status to those they wanted to impress.

During the 1820s, Sarah Vivian ran a 'Dame school' in the building. Industrialists like the Vivians considered schooling of the working classes essential for industry's ongoing success. However, state schooling did not become universally available for another 50 years. Until then, the industrialists lobbied the government for change and provided their own schooling. Dame schools were usually run by women without professional teaching qualifications and focused on teaching basic literacy and numeracy alongside moral and social values. The latter may be why the building sports the motto '*LEBE SO DASS DU WIEDER LEBEN MAGST*' – 'live so that you may live again'. The other motto, '*LIBERTE ET PATRIE*', means 'liberty and fatherland' and is featured on the flag of Vaud, one of the Swiss cantons.

Many Swiss-style cottages from this era have not survived the ravages of time, and this one has only just done so. A fire in 2010, started by an arsonist, caused significant damage. The council repairs included a new roof, windows, doors, and stairs and a paint job completed in 2014. The result was a shiny, new-looking building, but after a decade or so of remaining empty, cuts to council budgets and competing priorities, the paint was peeling and the building unusable. A lease has been awarded to a developer for a café, hopefully giving one of Swansea's favourite places a new lease of life.

Address Singleton Park, Sketty, SA2 9DU | Getting there Several buses to Parc Beck or Sketty Cross; some parking near entrance to park on Gower Road | Tip Switzerland is famous for its chocolate. There are no Swiss chocolate shops in Swansea, but So Cocoa on Dunns Lane in Mumbles sells chocolates from around the world, including some hand made in Wales.

103 Swiss Valley Reservoir
Quenching Llanelli's thirst

Considering the amount of 'liquid sunshine' that falls on Wales, it would be easy to think that water supply is not an issue. However, a report produced in 1875 indicated that average life expectancy in the Llanelli area was less than 30 years, primarily due to the quantity and quality of water available to the townsfolk. The existing reservoir supplying the town was clearly not keeping up with the increasing demand caused by industrial growth. The powers that be were surprisingly quick to respond – three years later, a reservoir was opened in the Swiss Valley (Cwm Lliedi). The population and industrial demands for water continued to grow, so a second reservoir was opened.

When the River Lliedi proved too small to meet the still burgeoning requirements for water, more was pumped up from the Gwendraeth Fach. Eventually, even this was not enough, and today the drinking water for Llanelli comes from Llyn Brianne, high up on the River Tywi. Water from the Swiss Valley reservoirs is still used by the Trostre steel works, but their requirements are reducing thanks to water conservation measures.

In addition to their crucial role in supplying water, the Swiss Valley reservoirs have become important wildlife habitats, supporting a diverse array of flora and fauna. The preservation of these natural assets has become an integral part of the reservoirs' management, ensuring that they continue to serve as vital ecosystems and green space for the community. In 2020, Llanelli Rural Council made a community adoption agreement with Welsh Water so they could turn the reservoir into a real asset for local people. It now has a good-quality path all the way around and provides facilities for recreational water activities such as paddleboarding and kayaking. This includes a changing spaces facility with hoist and a kayak launch platform for wheelchair users.

Address Swiss Valley, Llanelli, SA14 8ES, www.llanelli-rural.gov.uk/your-community/swiss-valley-reservoir | Getting there Bus 128 to Danylan, then a 10-minute walk; car park on site | Hours Reservoir unrestricted; car park daily 9am–8pm | Tip A list of sports clubs that have met InSport standards for provision that includes people with disabilities can be found on the Disability Sport Wales website (www.disabilitysportwales.com/en-gb/join-in).

104 Townhill Jewish Cemetery
A congregation's journey

As Swansea no longer has a synagogue, it is easy to forget how large a Jewish population the city once had. The Swansea congregation is the earliest in Wales, founded almost 300 years ago. The first synagogue, built from wood, was erected in 1740. The population of Jews in Swansea remained at a few hundred for a couple of centuries. Over time, several synagogues came and went, and at one point, there were two.

Between 1880 and 1920, the Russian Empire persecuted Jews, and this led to a huge exodus. The timing coincided with industrial growth in Swansea and the consequent need for goods and services, which refugees were well placed to provide. It was, therefore, a popular city for Jews to move to, and the population rose to around 1,000. During this period, Jewish society flourished in the city.

As industry declined, so did the attractiveness of Swansea. Young Jews moved away, which meant that few were raising families here. The pattern continued as young people sought cities with a more vibrant Jewish community in which to live. In 1941, the main synagogue on Goat Street was hit by a Nazi bomb during the three-day raid that flattened much of the city. It was replaced with a modern building on Ffynone Road in 1955. The population of Jews in Swansea continued to shrink, and by 2009, the congregation was too small to maintain a place of worship. The building is now used by the Life-Point Church, and the Jewish congregation meets in one of its rooms.

The Jewish congregation was granted a plot of land to use as a burial ground in 1768, making Townhill the oldest Jewish cemetery in Wales. The cemetery was officially closed in 1965 when it was full, and Swansea Jews are now interred at Oystermouth Cemetery instead. The gates to Townhill Cemetery are usually locked, although some of the headstones are visible through the bars.

Address High View, Mayhill, Swansea, SA1 6US | Getting there Several buses to Zoar Chapel followed by a 10-minute uphill walk; on-street parking opposite entrance | Hours Viewable through the gates only | Tip Nearby Bry-y-don Park has a playground with fantastic views over the city and bay. The entrance is about 80 metres down High View.

105 Ty'n-yr-Heol Depot
Where locks came to life

The Neath Canal was built during the Industrial Revolution to connect coal mines and foundries. Its construction took great ingenuity and determination from the 18th-century engineers and hardworking 'navvies' who brought it to life. Engineers had to survey the route and calculate the precise gradients to ensure proper water flow. Teams of skilled Irish labourers earned the nickname 'navvies' from their work on these navigation canals. Many of the same men went on to construct the railways and retained the nickname.

One critical component of the canal's infrastructure was the locks, which allowed boats to negotiate changes in gradient while maintaining the water at a navigable depth. Ty'n-yr-Heol depot was established to facilitate the construction and maintenance of the locks. It was a hive of activity, housing a timber shed, sawmill and smithy. The sawmill cut the wood to size, while the smithy crafted the ironwork for the lock gates. A block and tackle system was used to manoeuvre the heavy gates. Across the canal, the canal manager's house and stables stood watch over the operations and still stand today.

From its opening in 1795, the Neath Canal thrived for nearly half a century, transporting up to 200,000 tonnes of coal annually, along with a wide array of materials essential to the Industrial Revolution. Its cargo ranged from iron and ironstone to bricks, silica and even 15 cannons destined for the Napoleonic War in 1812.

However, the canal's heyday was relatively short-lived – it only thrived for around 50 years before starting to decline. By 1921, it had become obsolete, and it officially closed in 1934. Although it still contains water, the canal and its locks are no longer maintained. However, it retains its towpath for around 10 kilometres (6.5 miles), offering a delightful, easy walking route and a haven for wildlife.

Address Tonna, Neath, SA11 3DZ | Getting there Several buses to Lock Hill; on-street parking nearby | Hours Unrestricted | Tip Although the canal is no longer navigable, it is possible to take boat trips along the River Tawe from central Swansea on the Copper Jack, a boat owned by the Swansea Community Boat Trust (www.scbt.org.uk).

106 Vernon Watkins' Workplace

Bank clerk, code-breaker and poet

Vernon Watkins had a shaky start to his life. He was born on 27 June, 1906, the day that South Wales shook to the vibrations of an earthquake that reached 5.2 on the Richter scale. Swansea is on two geological fault lines, so it is more prone to earthquakes than most places in the British Isles. However, earthquakes of any intensity remain few and far between, and this one, although only moderate, remains notable, even though it happened more than a century ago.

Despite the drama on the day of his birth, Vernon Watkins was a quiet and steady man. His life was in total contrast to that of his friend and fellow poet Dylan Thomas, who led the high life. Vernon Watkins spent 38 years working as a teller in the Lloyds Bank branch that once stood at 77 St Helen's Road. The stability of his work gave him the time and energy to write his poetry for hours every night. This resulted in an extensive collection of work published either in books of his own or in anthologies. Vernon Watkins' tendency to lead a quiet life did not give him the high profile of more notorious poets, either during his lifetime or after his death. Many believe, however, that this is not a reflection of the quality of his poetry.

For three years during World War II, Vernon Watkins became a cryptographer at Bletchley Park, where the brightest minds in Britain were pitted against the coded messages being transmitted by the Germans.

Although the bank has long since left 77 St Helen's Road, the vault in the basement remains, now empty of valuables, but still with a pair of safes that have proved too difficult to remove. Considering Vernon Watkins' time spent as a code-breaker, perhaps it is appropriate that his main workplace is now a board game café where people are intellectually pitted against each other.

Address Common Meeple Board Game Café, 77 St Helen's Road, Swansea, SA1 4BG, +44 (0)1792 304898, www.commonmeeple.co.uk | Getting there Several buses to St Helen's Road or Beach Street; on-street parking nearby | Hours Wed–Mon 10am–11pm | Tip A few metres back along St Helen's Road, Exotica sells a wide range of food from around the world (Facebook group: Exotica Foods Swansea).

107 — Volcano Theatre

An eruption of creativity

The large, spray-painted mural of Elizabeth Taylor in tears that adorns the grey frontage of the Volcano Theatre has become a bit of a landmark in Swansea. It was painted by Charles Uzzell Edwards (AKA Pure Evil), an artist who has created similar portraits of several film stars crying, including the Welsh icons Richard Burton, Catherine Zeta-Jones and Anthony Hopkins. The artist, who grew up in Swansea, chose Elizabeth Taylor as his subject for this portrait because he was fascinated by her relationship with Richard Burton and how that linked her to South Wales.

If you enter the Volcano Theatre expecting a traditional stage and auditorium, you will be surprised. It is based in a disused shop, and between shows, has all the romance that promises. However, this also means that the space is flexible and lends itself to immersive and unusual theatre. It allows playwrights to be more imaginative – and playful – in their approach. The audience can move between small rooms, sit around cabaret-style tables or just face the stage as usual. Rather than just the stage, the whole theatre can be dressed for the performance, and the Volcano Theatre staff will work with playwrights to fulfil their creative ambitions wherever possible.

The theatre produces a variety of projects, and tours its shows around the UK and beyond. It also hosts other touring companies when they visit South Wales. The theatre is experimental and helps other people – both youth and adult – to bring out their creativity. The 'Storyopolis' project based at the theatre uses creativity to help build literacy for disadvantaged children. There is also an art gallery on site that the public can drop into.

The Elizabeth Taylor mural is one of several adornments to buildings on the High Street, most of which are brighter and more cheerful, and some of which cover the entire frontage of the buildings they decorate.

Address 27–29 High Street, Swansea, SA1 1LG, +44 (0)1792 464790, www.volcanotheatre.wales, mail@volcanotheatre.co.uk | Getting there Close to Swansea railway station; several buses run up the High Street; nearest parking at NCP Swansea Orchard Street | Hours Tue–Sat 10am–5pm | Tip For more murals, head to Llanelli, where local man Steve Jenkins (AKA 'Jenks') has painted many walls.

108__ Votes for Women
'No Persons Here'

By the early 20th century, women began to demand that they be given voting rights on an equal footing with men. This was known as 'suffrage', and there were three leading campaigning organisations in Wales. The National Union of Suffrage Societies (NUSS) was a suffragist organisation that believed in peaceful and lawful campaigning. The Women's Social and Political Union (WSPU) was a suffragette organisation that believed that violent direct action was required. Its members launched increasingly violent attacks, and its members were often imprisoned for their actions. The Women's Freedom League (WFL) sat somewhere between the two. Its members were willing to break the law to achieve their aims but would not engage in violence.

Clara Neal was the headteacher at Terrace Road Primary School for 20 years. Today, there is a blue plaque here commemorating her role as a founding – and active – member of the Women's Freedom League's Swansea branch. This came to be the dominant suffrage group in the town. Women in the movement were always looking for ways to raise the profile of their cause, and the 1911 Census provided an opportunity to do so. Across England and Wales, activist women disrupted the census in different ways, flummoxing the enumerators. Some held parties and moved from house to house to make counting and recording difficult. Others refused to give their details on the census forms, instead making notes such as 'No persons here, only women', and, 'As women don't count, they refuse to be counted'. Clara Neal was among those who spent the night outdoors to avoid being counted, hiding in a cave with several female friends.

Despite the distraction of World War I, the battle for equality gained ground in 1918, when women over 30 and meeting certain property qualifications were permitted to vote. Still, it took another 10 years for full suffrage to finally be achieved.

Address Terrace Road Primary School, opposite 113 Norfolk Street, Swansea, SA1 6JB |
Getting there Bus 49 to Constitution Hill; parking on Norfolk Street | Hours Unrestricted |
Tip The limestone cliffs of Gower are riddled with caves (most of which are best approached
at low tide). The most impressive is perhaps Culver Hole near Port Eynon, with its stone
blockwork wall in front of the cave (www.ogof.org.uk/areas/south-gower-coast-caves.html).

109_Weobley Castle

A steward's stronghold

David de la Bere's position as Steward to the Lord of Gower granted him significant influence and wealth, enabling him to acquire the land on which he would build Weobley Castle at the turn of the 14th century. The castle was constructed primarily as a comfortable manor house in which to entertain guests. However, it still has several defensive features, such as a watchtower and crenelated wall-tops, that would have provided a degree of protection from attack.

During their heyday, Norman castles like this were not the stark, gloomy stone buildings devoid of life we see today. Many were rendered and painted white or other light colours to make them more conspicuous. Now, Weobley Castle is barely visible from the other side of the estuary. When it was first built, it probably stood out like a beacon in the dark.

Most Norman castles provided homes to their owners within the fortifications. When the owner and his retinue were home, their halls and courtyards were bustling with servants, artisans, members of the household and guests. The clang of the blacksmith's hammer, the aroma of bread baking in the kitchens and the sounds of horses and livestock in the courtyard would have filled the air. Gatherings took place in the main hall; private meetings were held in bedrooms with sitting areas, known as 'solars'. The internal walls would also have been plastered, and some would have been painted with bright patterns. Tapestries on the walls provided multiple benefits, including heat insulation, sound muffling, another show of wealth and, of course, more decoration. In most castles, only faint remnants of this glorious past remain.

By the middle of the 17th century, 350 years after it was built, Weobley was in ruins and leased out, with neighbouring buildings being used as a farmhouse, much as they are today.

Address Swansea, SA3 1HB, www.cadw.gov.wales/visit/places-to-visit/weobley-castle |
Getting there Bus 115 and 116 to Greyhound Inn; some parking on site | **Hours** Apr–Oct
9.30am–6pm, Nov–Mar 9.30am–5pm | **Tip** The Britannia Inn at Llanmadoc is one of the
most popular pubs in the area. Choose between the cosy 17th-century bar with log burner
and the large garden with far-reaching views over the estuary (www.britanniagower.com).

110 Whitford Point Lighthouse

On the rocks

Whitford (also known as Whiteford) Point Lighthouse is a prominent feature visible from across Carmarthen Bay. Now that there are no major ports left along this stretch of coast, and the bay has silted up, it's hard to imagine how busy the waters here once were. Thousands of ships would visit Llanelli alone in a year, transporting ore into the metal smelting industries of the town and coal and goods out. The shifting sandbanks of the bay have always been treacherous, and numerous shipwrecks have been recorded in the area. Wrecks are visible at low tide on both Rhossili Beach and Cefn Sidan on the opposite side of the water.

The Whitford Point Lighthouse was built in 1865 to mark an area of shallow water at the north-western end of the Gower Peninsula. It is the only sizeable wave-swept iron tower left in Britain, rising more than 13 metres from the seabed. The tidal range here can be as great as 7.5 metres, and it stands in over 6 metres of water at high tide. The lighthouse is elegant, tapering from a broad base to the top. The construction is unusual because the cast-iron plates are bolted together from the outside, leaving ridges in the external face.

The lighthouse's base is just above sea level at low tide, so it is possible to walk out to it. When planning such a trip, you should check the tide times and leave plenty of time to return before the water rises. It is some distance from the nearest car park to the end of the land and a further half mile out to the lighthouse. The ground underfoot is uneven, damp in places, and difficult to negotiate without stepping on mussels. Please take care!

Whitford Point Lighthouse no longer houses a permanent lamp. However, it was lit on Queen Elizabeth II's Diamond Jubilee celebrations in 2022, when beacons shone across the country.

Address In the sea off Whiteford Point, near Cwm Ivy, SA3 1DJ | **Getting there** Car park at Cwm Ivy | **Hours** Accessible 24 hours | **Tip** Cwm Ivy Marsh, between the car park and the lighthouse, was claimed from the sea for grazing in the 17th century. In 2014, the sea wall was breached, and the National Trust allowed the land to revert to a tidal salt marsh. Now, it is a fully functioning wildlife habitat with a couple of hides for birdwatchers.

111 Woodland Burial Ground

A peaceful corner in Oystermouth Cemetery

For many people, being cremated at the end of their life is not an appealing option. This may stem from religious or cultural beliefs, a desire for their body to survive beyond death or, increasingly, concerns about the environmental impact of cremation. When cremating a body, the temperature must reach at least 800 degrees Celsius. This uses a lot of energy, generates carbon emissions and causes air pollution. The obvious alternative to cremation is to choose to be buried. Traditional burials in the UK often involve using a cocktail of chemicals to embalm the body and lining a coffin, which might not have been produced sustainably, with synthetic fabric. This has the effect of slowing down bodily decomposition and polluting the ground when it does decompose.

One alternative that has become popular is to choose a natural burial. No chemicals are used to prepare the body, and it is wrapped in a shroud or coffin that is sustainably produced and biodegradable. The graves themselves are usually on sites that are being managed for nature conservation, for example, in a woodland or a wildflower meadow. At natural burial sites, grave markers are usually subtle so they do not detract from the natural beauty of the place.

In Oystermouth Cemetery, most of the graves are traditional. Stone memorials march across the hillside in neat rows, surrounded by grass. However, in one corner, there is an altogether different space. This is a woodland burial ground where the graves are marked by carved wooden discs. Anyone can be buried here, whether religious or not. Trees surround areas of open space, which are managed to maximise their value to nature and grieving families. Here, families can listen to birdsong and watch bees buzzing around the flowers, knowing that their loved one remains a part of the cycle of life.

Address 94 Newton Road, Langland, Newton, Swansea, SA3 4SW, www.swansea.gov.uk |
Getting there Several buses go to Oystermouth Primary School, Langland Corner or
Southward Lane; parking on site during opening hours | Hours Accessible 24 hours for
pedestrians; vehicles Mon–Thu 9am–4.30pm, Fri 9am–4pm, Sat & Sun 10am–4pm | Tip
Oystermouth Cemetery also contains the graves of several lifeboat crew who have perished
while on duty, including those in the 1903 and 1947 disasters.

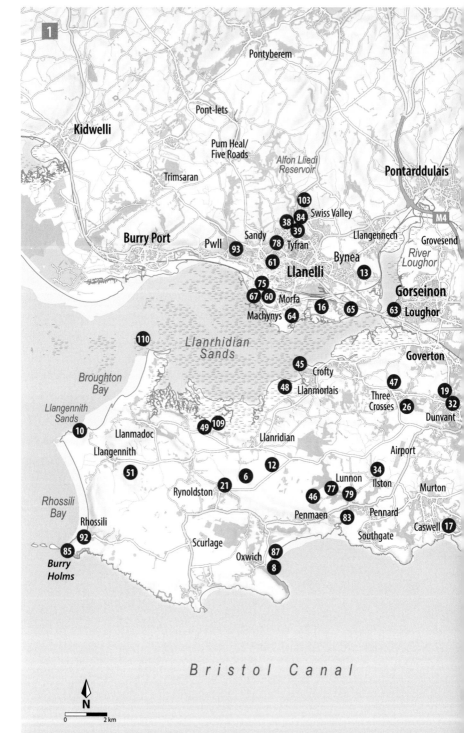

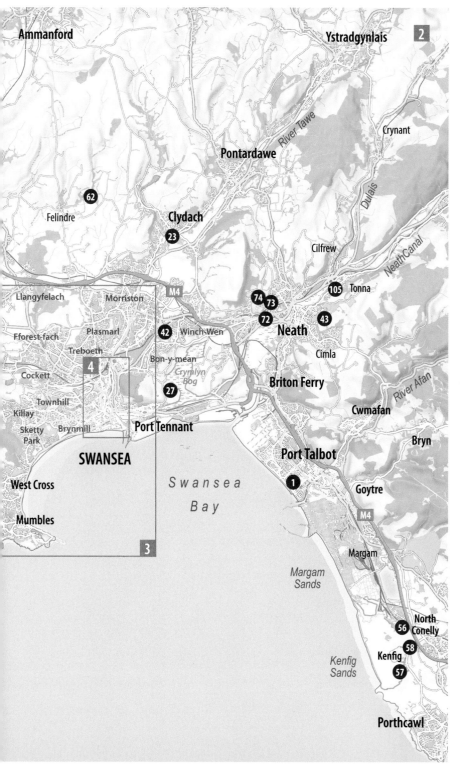

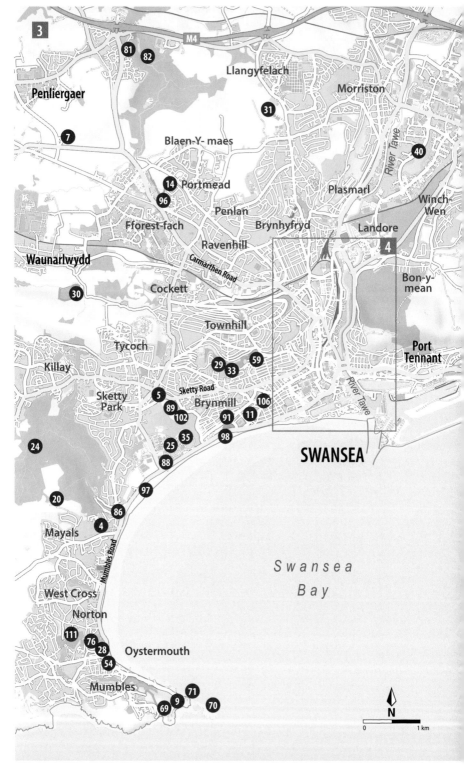

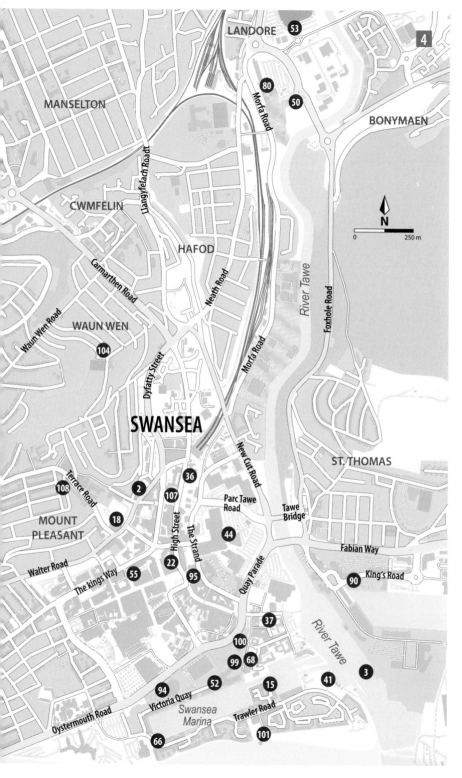

Catriona Neil, Adrian Spalding
**111 Places in Cornwall
That You Shouldn't Miss**
ISBN 978-3-7408-1901-9

Martin Booth, Barbara Evripidou
**111 Places in Bristol
That You Shouldn't Miss**
ISBN 978-3-7408-2001-5

Martin Booth, Barbara Evripidou
**111 Places for Kids in Bristol
That You Shouldn't Miss**
ISBN 978-3-7408-1665-0

Alexandra Loske
**111 Places in Brighton and
Lewes That You Shouldn't Miss**
ISBN 978-3-7408-1727-5

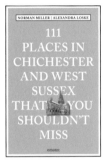

Norman Miller, Alexandra Loske
**111 Places in Chichester
and West Sussex
That You Shouldn't Miss**
ISBN 978-3-7408-1784-8

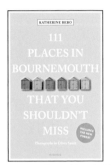

Katherine Bebo, Oliver Smith
**111 Places in Bournemouth
That You Shouldn't Miss**
ISBN 978-3-7408-1166-2

Ben Waddington, Janet Hart
**111 Places in Birmingham
That You Shouldn't Miss**
ISBN 978-3-7408-2268-2

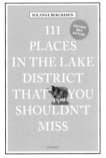

Solange Berchemin
**111 Places in the Lake District
That You Shouldn't Miss**
ISBN 978-3-7408-1861-6

Ed Glinert, David Taylor
**111 Places in Oxford
That You Shouldn't Miss**
ISBN 978-3-7408-1990-3

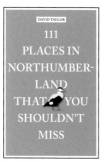

David Taylor
**111 Places in Northumberland
That You Shouldn't Miss**
ISBN 978-3-7408-1792-3

Ed Glinert, David Taylor
**111 Places in Yorkshire
That You Shouldn't Miss**
ISBN 978-3-7408-1167-9

Ed Glinert, Karin Tearle
**111 Places in Essex
That You Shouldn't Miss**
ISBN 978-3-7408-1593-6

John Sykes, Birgit Weber
**111 Places in London
That You Shouldn't Miss**
ISBN 978-3-7408-2379-5

Alicia Edwards
**111 Places for Kids in London
That You Shouldn't Miss**
ISBN 978-3-7408-2196-8

Michael Glover, Benedict Flett
**111 Hidden Art Treasures
in London That You Shouldn't
Miss**
ISBN 978-3-7408-1576-9

Terry Philpot, Karin Tearle
**111 Literary Places in London
That You Shouldn't Miss**
ISBN 978-3-7408-1954-5

Jonjo Maudsley, James Riley
**111 Places in Windsor
That You Shouldn't Miss**
ISBN 978-3-7408-2009-1

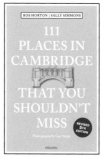

Rosalind Horton,
Sally Simmons, Guy Snape
**111 Places in Cambridge
That You Shouldn't Miss**
ISBN 978-3-7408-1285-0

Phil Lee, Rachel Ghent
111 Places in Nottingham
That You Shouldn't Miss
ISBN 978-3-7408-2261-3

Cath Muldowney
111 Places in Bradford
That You Shouldn't Miss
ISBN 978-3-7408-1427-4

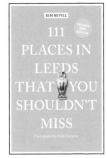

Kim Revill, Alesh Compton
111 Places in Leeds
That You Shouldn't Miss
ISBN 978-3-7408-0754-2

Michael Glover,
Richard Anderson
111 Places in Sheffield
That You Shouldn't Miss
ISBN 978-3-7408-2348-1

Julian Treuherz,
Peter de Figueiredo
111 Places in Manchester
That You Shouldn't Miss
ISBN 978-3-7408-2246-0

Julian Treuherz,
Peter de Figueiredo
111 Places in Liverpool
That You Shouldn't Miss
ISBN 978-3-7408-1607-0

Gillian Tait
111 Places in Edinburgh
That You Shouldn't Miss
ISBN 978-3-7408-1476-2

Tom Shields, Gillian Tait
111 Places in Glasgow
That You Shouldn't Miss
ISBN 978-3-7408-2237-8

Gillian Tait
111 Places in Fife
That You Shouldn't Miss
ISBN 978-3-7408-0597-5

Acknowledgements

So many people have helped me in my quest to create a memorable experience for readers of this book that it is not possible to mention everyone individually. If you are one of them, then please know how grateful I am for your help and support.

I want to extend thanks to the Outdoor Writers and Photographers Guild, of which I am a member. It was at an OWPG event that I first saw one of the '111 Places' books, written and photographed by David Taylor. It was beautiful. I loved the concept, style and quality of the book. I was hooked; I wanted to write one of my own. Without that book, I might still be in the dark about this wonderful series, so thank you, David. Without Laura Olk's faith in me, this book would never have got off the starting blocks, and without Tania Taylor's meticulous editing, it would be nowhere near as good as it is – thank you both.

Writing a book is not an easy endeavour – it takes a massive amount of time, effort and attention. Therefore, my final and biggest thank you is to my husband, Mike, who consistently provides me with the support and encouragement I need in my authoring life.

Julia Goodfellow-Smith loved her life in the Midlands, but it was missing one important thing; the sea. On arriving in Llanelli, she and her husband started exploring – and found unexpected treasures. In this book, she shares her love of the area and some of the best things she found.

The information in this book was accurate at the time of publication, but it can change at any time. Please confirm the details for the places you're planning to visit before you head out on your adventures.